Praise for *My Mom Had an Abortion*

"It's a rare gift to be welcomed into the inner corridors of a person's life, especially a person as frank, funny, and utterly allergic to posturing as Beezus B. Murphy. You have to admire Beezus's clarity of self and her warm curiosity about the hard things as she writes her way through them. Beezus approaches abortion and periods and sexuality with the vulnerable authenticity of a young person actively hashing these issues out in real time—which, of course, she is. The fact that she feels free to be so free, because she never really learned that she wasn't supposed to talk about these things, is one of the most hopeful sights our currently very unfree universe has to offer."
—Lindy West, author of *Shrill*

"Beezus B. Murphy's graphic novel is thoughtful, honest, blunt, and smart. We don't talk openly enough about this subject, and Ms. Murphy does so in such a conversational way that you kind of forget it's supposed to be taboo. I won't forget this one."
—Dana Simpson, author and illustrator of *Phoebe and Her Unicorn*

"Beezus B. Murphy's writing brims with curiosity, generosity, and precocious wisdom. She candidly and expertly presents the complexities of learning how to distinguish between stereotypes and what really is, and how one eloquent teen views the social repercussions of our culture's representation of the female reproductive system. Tatiana Gill's friendly, straightforward artwork is perfectly matched with the text. The reader can easily imagine Beezus and Tatiana having intimate, animated conversations and really getting a kick out of each other. Like Beezus, I wouldn't exist if it weren't for my mom's abortion. It's a complicated, powerful thing to know, and we both remain amazed and thankful. Our moms' decisions weren't easy, but they allowed them to live their own rewarding lives—which eventually included loving relationships with us!"
—Ellen Forney, artist and author

D1307964

"Beezus B. Murphy's *My Mom Had an Abortion* has more real-but-not-precious, raw-but-not-wrenching stories packed into its relatively few pages than you'd imagine it could. It's full of poignant, funny, and empathetic connective thread between generations and families, mothers and daughters, reproductive experience and autonomy, growing up, sexual identity, and more, all in Beezus's deeply original, open, and accessible voice that feels both warmly familiar and wholly original. Tatiana Gill's down-to-earth illustrations add the perfect touch to this unique addition to the next generation of powerful proabortion lit."
—Heather Corinna, founder of Scarleteen, author of *S.E.X.: The All-You-Need-to-Know Sexuality Guide to Get You Through Your Teens and Twenties* and *What Fresh Hell Is This? Perimenopause, Menopause, Other Indignities, and You*

"A vital, honest representation of a proven but consistently overlooked fact—the majority of people who have had abortions are parents. By showing an honest conversation between mom and daughter, *My Mom Had an Abortion* shows the lingering effects of stigma, the power of storytelling, and the myriad of reproductive and pregnancy outcomes and experiences that are demonized to the detriment of those who experience them. A loving reminder that abortion is often a parenting decision that makes it possible for people to grow their families when they're willing, ready, and able, this is required reading for anyone who knows and loves someone who has had an abortion. Yes, this means you."
—Danielle Campoamor, writer, editor, and abortion advocate

"Who wrote the rule that you have to be an adult to publish a book? Thanks to teenager Beezus B. Murphy, illustrator Tatiana Gill, Shout Your Abortion, and PM Press, we get this marvelous autobiographical graphic novel about a young lesbian growing up in Seattle. Beezus's tender honesty gives you the feeling that you are sitting around chatting with a close friend, opening up to each other about school challenges, pop culture's influence on your beliefs, and puberty. I hope this isn't Beezus's last book, because I want to read more!"
—Jacinta Bunnell, author of *A More Graceful Shaboom*

"Sixteen-year-old Beezus B. Murphy writes with a whip-smart self-awareness that gives me hope for America's future. With a deft balance of insight and humor, *My Mom Had an Abortion* is a warm and welcome demonstration of how we can—and should!—talk about abortion as a normal and vital human right."
—Tessa Hulls, author of forthcoming graphic novel *Feeding Ghosts*

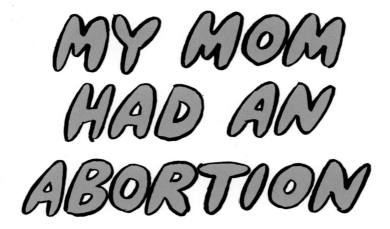

MY MOM HAD AN ABORTION

A Shout Your Abortion Project

Words by **Beezus B. Murphy**

Drawn by **Tatiana Gill**

Postscript by **Amelia Bonow**

My Mom Had an Abortion
© Beezus B. Murphy and Tatiana Gill
This edition © 2022 PM Press

ISBN: 978–1–62963–913–0 (paperback)
ISBN: 978–1–629639–222 (ebook)
Library of Congress Control Number: 2021936603

10 9 8 7 6 5 4 3 2 1

PM Press
PO Box 23912
Oakland, CA 94623
www.pmpress.org

Printed in the USA.

Dedication and Acknowledgments

I dedicate this graphic novel to my parents Shawna and Christian, who have always supported and believed in me, even when I didn't believe in myself. To my sister Minnow, who has always managed to bring sunshine and joy into my life. To my sister Elena for being my constant companion as a child and showing me how to truly love life. To my kindergarten teacher Jennifer Nieman for giving me such a strong start to my education. To my third/fourth-grade teacher Roman Gluckman for always pushing me to do my best. To resource room teacher Ms. Rook for finally teaching me how to read. To my best friend Hazel for helping me realize that I wasn't alone, and that there were people out there who understood me. I just needed to know where to look. To my amazing illustrator Tatiana Gill, whose artwork truly brought my journey to life. And, finally, to the greats, Allison Bechdel, Raina Telgemeier, and Maia Kobabe, who were all hugely inspirational for me in both my writing of this book and in my life overall.

Sincerely,
Beezus

CHAPTER 1:

WHAT?!

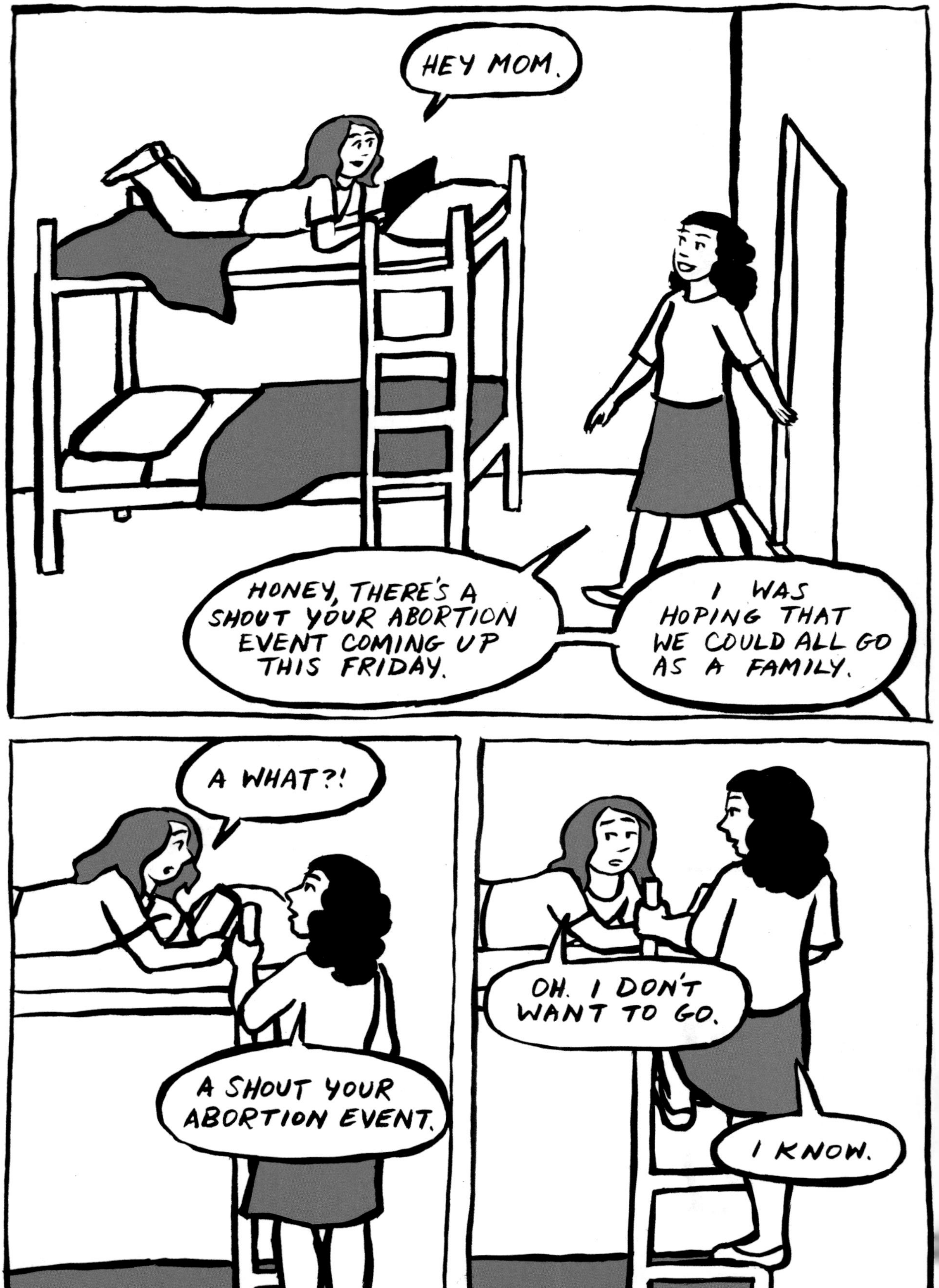
HEY MOM.
HONEY, THERE'S A SHOUT YOUR ABORTION EVENT COMING UP THIS FRIDAY.
I WAS HOPING THAT WE COULD ALL GO AS A FAMILY.
A WHAT?!
A SHOUT YOUR ABORTION EVENT.
OH. I DON'T WANT TO GO.
I KNOW.

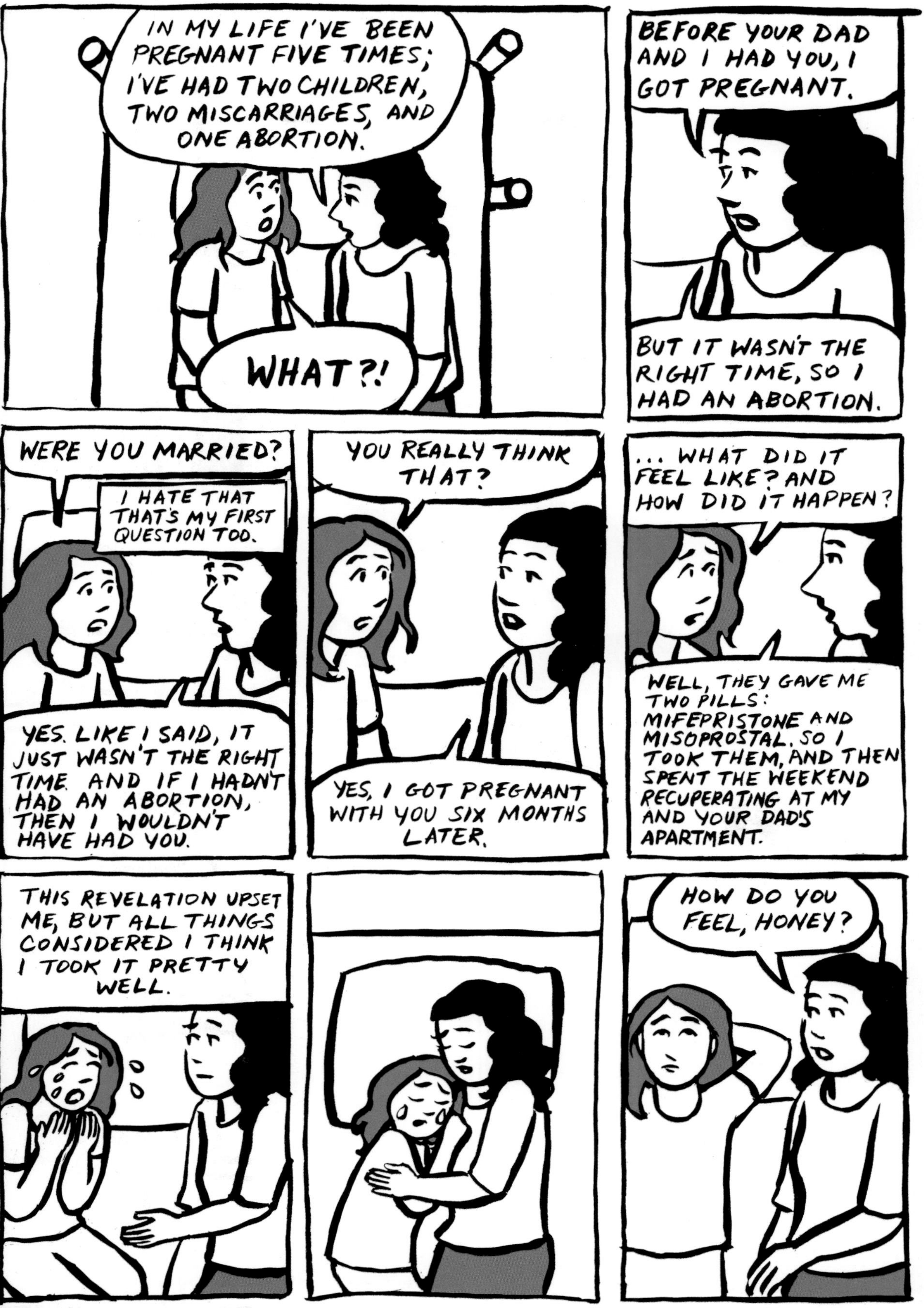
IN MY LIFE I'VE BEEN PREGNANT FIVE TIMES; I'VE HAD TWO CHILDREN, TWO MISCARRIAGES, AND ONE ABORTION.
WHAT?!
BEFORE YOUR DAD AND I HAD YOU, I GOT PREGNANT.
BUT IT WASN'T THE RIGHT TIME, SO I HAD AN ABORTION.
WERE YOU MARRIED?
I HATE THAT THAT'S MY FIRST QUESTION TOO.
YES. LIKE I SAID, IT JUST WASN'T THE RIGHT TIME. AND IF I HADN'T HAD AN ABORTION, THEN I WOULDN'T HAVE HAD YOU.
YOU REALLY THINK THAT?
YES, I GOT PREGNANT WITH YOU SIX MONTHS LATER.
... WHAT DID IT FEEL LIKE? AND HOW DID IT HAPPEN?
WELL, THEY GAVE ME TWO PILLS: MIFEPRISTONE AND MISOPROSTAL. SO I TOOK THEM, AND THEN SPENT THE WEEKEND RECUPERATING AT MY AND YOUR DAD'S APARTMENT.
THIS REVELATION UPSET ME, BUT ALL THINGS CONSIDERED I THINK I TOOK IT PRETTY WELL.
HOW DO YOU FEEL, HONEY?

CHAPTER 2:

SO, HOW DO I FEEL?

OKAY, NOW LET'S BACK UP A BIT; MY VIEWPOINT OF ABORTION
WAS LARGELY SHAPED BY OUTSIDE SOURCES. MY FIRST
EXPOSURE TO ABORTION WAS ON THIS REALLY AWFUL
TEEN DRAMA I WATCHED WHEN I WAS LIKE 11, 'THE
SECRET LIFE OF THE AMERICAN TEENAGER,' WHICH I ONLY
WATCHED BECAUSE MOLLY RINGWALD PLAYED THE MAIN
CHARACTER'S MOM. ANYWAY, THE PROTAGONIST AMY GOT
PREGNANT FROM HAVING SEX WITH THIS GUY RICKY THAT SHE
MET AT BAND CAMP, BUT HE ALREADY HAD AN ON-AGAIN,
OFF-AGAIN GIRLFRIEND NAMED ADRIAN. SO AMY WANTED TO
GET AN ABORTION, BUT THEN THIS OTHER GIRL THAT
RICKY WAS SORT OF SEEING, GRACE, WHO WAS A CONSERVATIVE
CHRISTIAN, DIDN'T WANT HER TO GET ONE SO SHE WENT TO
THE CLINIC AND CONVINCED AMY NOT TO. EVEN THOUGH IT
WAS WHAT BOTH AMY AND RICKY WANTED AND IT REALLY
WASN'T GRACE'S PLACE TO INTERVENE. AND GET THIS,
SHE EVEN SAID:

DON'T WORRY,
RICKY. I WON'T
LET ANYTHING
HAPPEN TO YOUR
BABY.

AND GRACE IS ACTUALLY TREATED AS IN THE RIGHT FOR DOING
THIS! EVEN LOOKING BACK ON IT NOW IT JUST MAKES ME
MAD. WHILE THAT WASN'T THE FIRST OR ONLY TEEN DRAMA I
EVER WATCHED, IT WAS DEFINITELY THE WORST.

AND THIS SHOW WASN'T THE ONLY SHOW THAT SPREAD THIS MESSAGE. THE PREGNANT TEENAGER CLICHÉ IS LUDICROUSLY PREVALENT IN POP CULTURE. BUT THOSE GIRLS NEVER GET ABORTIONS BECAUSE THEN THE PLOTLINE WOULD BE OVER. THAT'S WHY I LIKED HOW 'JUNO,' DESPITE THE FACT THAT JUNO ULTIMATELY DECIDED TO GIVE HER BABY UP FOR ADOPTION, DIDN'T PAINT ABORTION IN A NEGATIVE LIGHT. IT JUST WASN'T THE RIGHT CHOICE FOR HER. PEOPLE SHOULDN'T BE SHAMED FOR GETTING OR NOT GETTING ABORTIONS. YOUNG PEOPLE ABSORB THE INFORMATION THAT WE GATHER FROM OUR SURROUNDINGS — SOMETIMES IT'S GOOD INFORMATION, AND OTHER TIMES IT CAN BE HARMFUL. AND THERE ARE TONS OF KIDS WHO THINK ABORTION IS MURDER, LIKE I USED TO, JUST BECAUSE SOMEONE OR SOMETHING ELSE TOLD THEM SO. I HAVEN'T ALWAYS FELT THIS WAY — FOR MY ENTIRE DECADE AND A HALF OF EXISTENCE — BUT NOW I REALIZE ABORTION IS PERFECTLY NORMAL AND SHOULD BE KEPT SAFE AND LEGAL. I ALSO THINK THAT IT'S IMPORTANT FOR PEOPLE TO EDUCATE THEMSELVES ABOUT IT TO REDUCE THE STIGMA SURROUNDING IT. EVEN THOUGH THERE ARE PLENTY OF GRACES IN THE WORLD WHO THINK OTHERWISE.

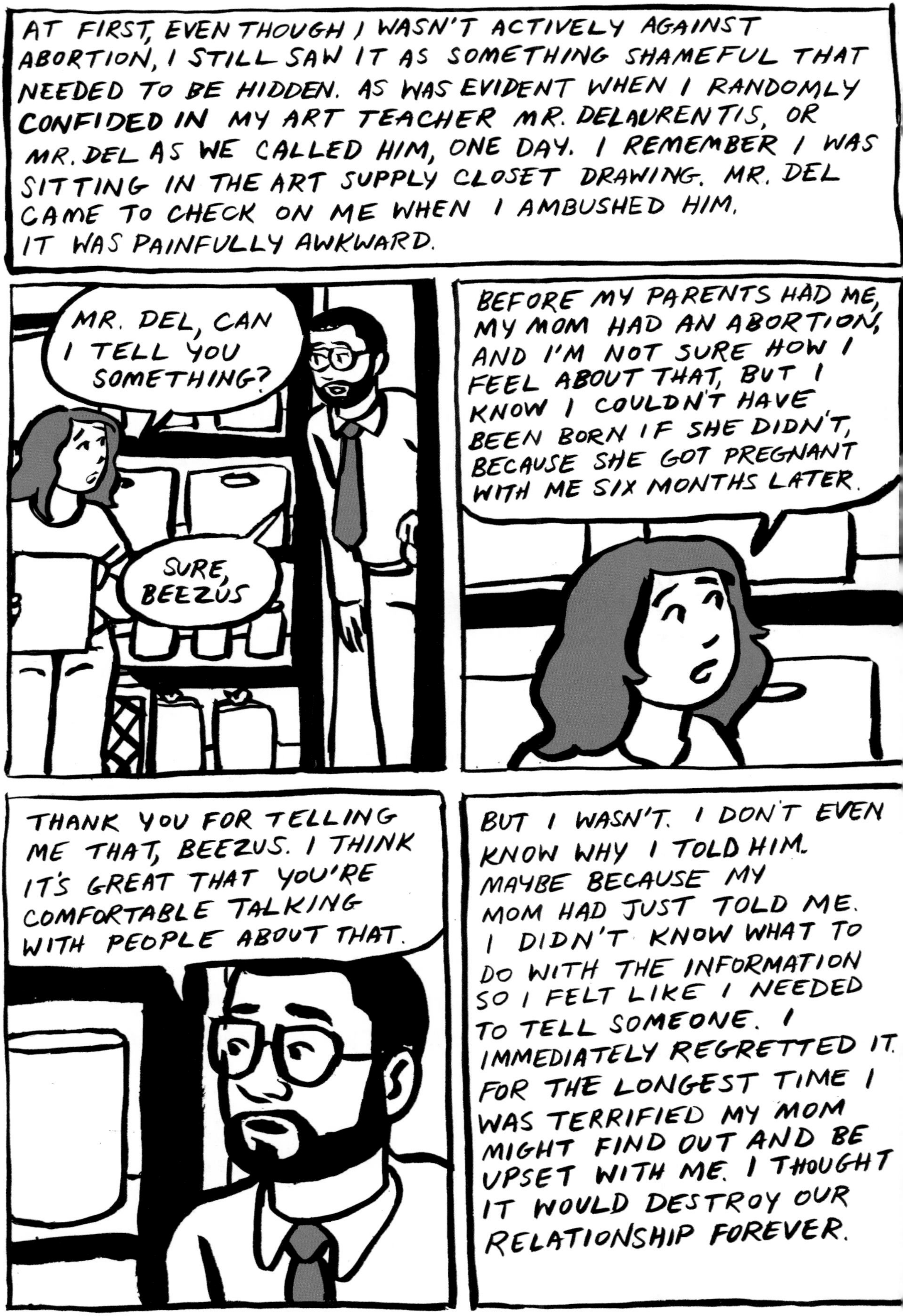
AT FIRST, EVEN THOUGH I WASN'T ACTIVELY AGAINST ABORTION, I STILL SAW IT AS SOMETHING SHAMEFUL THAT NEEDED TO BE HIDDEN. AS WAS EVIDENT WHEN I RANDOMLY CONFIDED IN MY ART TEACHER MR. DELAURENTIS, OR MR. DEL AS WE CALLED HIM, ONE DAY. I REMEMBER I WAS SITTING IN THE ART SUPPLY CLOSET DRAWING. MR. DEL CAME TO CHECK ON ME WHEN I AMBUSHED HIM. IT WAS PAINFULLY AWKWARD.
MR. DEL, CAN I TELL YOU SOMETHING?
SURE, BEEZUS
BEFORE MY PARENTS HAD ME, MY MOM HAD AN ABORTION, AND I'M NOT SURE HOW I FEEL ABOUT THAT, BUT I KNOW I COULDN'T HAVE BEEN BORN IF SHE DIDN'T, BECAUSE SHE GOT PREGNANT WITH ME SIX MONTHS LATER.
THANK YOU FOR TELLING ME THAT, BEEZUS. I THINK IT'S GREAT THAT YOU'RE COMFORTABLE TALKING WITH PEOPLE ABOUT THAT.
BUT I WASN'T. I DON'T EVEN KNOW WHY I TOLD HIM. MAYBE BECAUSE MY MOM HAD JUST TOLD ME. I DIDN'T KNOW WHAT TO DO WITH THE INFORMATION SO I FELT LIKE I NEEDED TO TELL SOMEONE. I IMMEDIATELY REGRETTED IT. FOR THE LONGEST TIME I WAS TERRIFIED MY MOM MIGHT FIND OUT AND BE UPSET WITH ME. I THOUGHT IT WOULD DESTROY OUR RELATIONSHIP FOREVER.

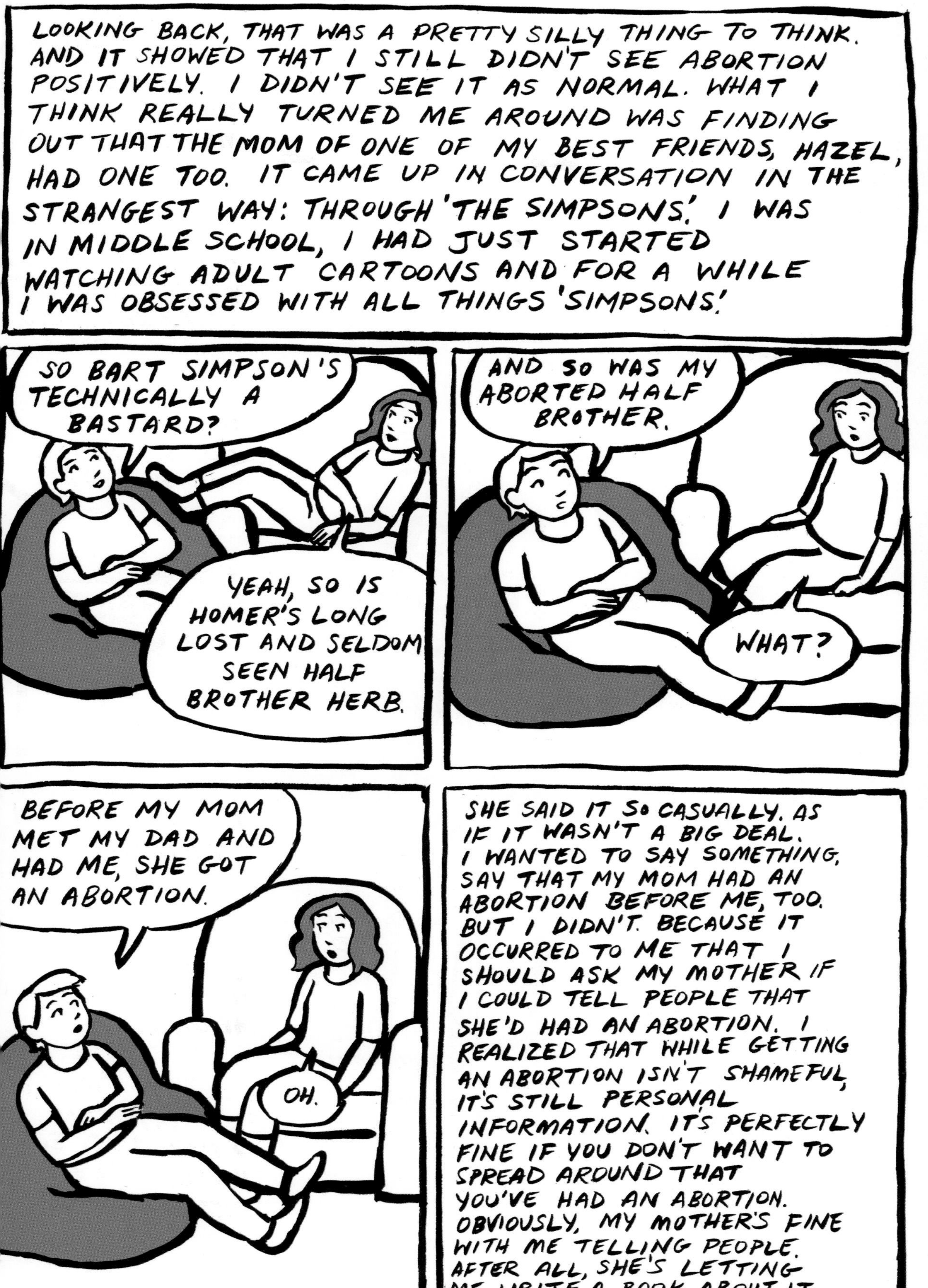
LOOKING BACK, THAT WAS A PRETTY SILLY THING TO THINK. AND IT SHOWED THAT I STILL DIDN'T SEE ABORTION POSITIVELY. I DIDN'T SEE IT AS NORMAL. WHAT I THINK REALLY TURNED ME AROUND WAS FINDING OUT THAT THE MOM OF ONE OF MY BEST FRIENDS, HAZEL, HAD ONE TOO. IT CAME UP IN CONVERSATION IN THE STRANGEST WAY: THROUGH 'THE SIMPSONS.' I WAS IN MIDDLE SCHOOL, I HAD JUST STARTED WATCHING ADULT CARTOONS AND FOR A WHILE I WAS OBSESSED WITH ALL THINGS 'SIMPSONS.'
SO BART SIMPSON'S TECHNICALLY A BASTARD?
YEAH, SO IS HOMER'S LONG LOST AND SELDOM SEEN HALF BROTHER HERB.
AND SO WAS MY ABORTED HALF BROTHER.
WHAT?
BEFORE MY MOM MET MY DAD AND HAD ME, SHE GOT AN ABORTION.
OH.
SHE SAID IT SO CASUALLY. AS IF IT WASN'T A BIG DEAL. I WANTED TO SAY SOMETHING, SAY THAT MY MOM HAD AN ABORTION BEFORE ME, TOO. BUT I DIDN'T. BECAUSE IT OCCURRED TO ME THAT I SHOULD ASK MY MOTHER IF I COULD TELL PEOPLE THAT SHE'D HAD AN ABORTION. I REALIZED THAT WHILE GETTING AN ABORTION ISN'T SHAMEFUL, IT'S STILL PERSONAL INFORMATION. IT'S PERFECTLY FINE IF YOU DON'T WANT TO SPREAD AROUND THAT YOU'VE HAD AN ABORTION. OBVIOUSLY, MY MOTHER'S FINE WITH ME TELLING PEOPLE. AFTER ALL, SHE'S LETTING ME WRITE A BOOK ABOUT IT.

CHAPTER 3:
OF MOMS AND MISCARRIAGES

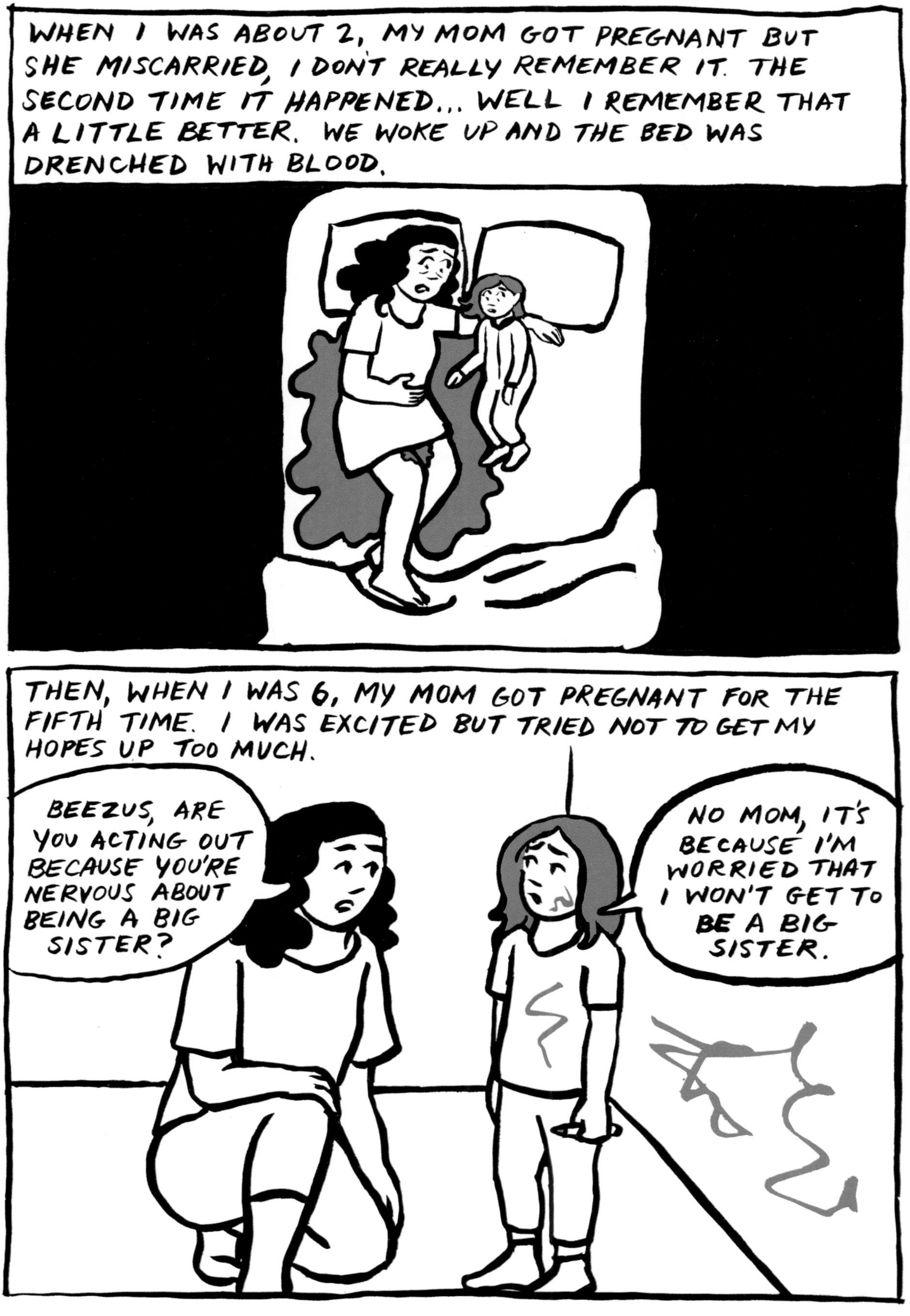
WHEN I WAS ABOUT 2, MY MOM GOT PREGNANT BUT SHE MISCARRIED, I DON'T REALLY REMEMBER IT. THE SECOND TIME IT HAPPENED... WELL I REMEMBER THAT A LITTLE BETTER. WE WOKE UP AND THE BED WAS DRENCHED WITH BLOOD.
THEN, WHEN I WAS 6, MY MOM GOT PREGNANT FOR THE FIFTH TIME. I WAS EXCITED BUT TRIED NOT TO GET MY HOPES UP TOO MUCH.
BEEZUS, ARE YOU ACTING OUT BECAUSE YOU'RE NERVOUS ABOUT BEING A BIG SISTER?
NO MOM, IT'S BECAUSE I'M WORRIED THAT I WON'T GET TO BE A BIG SISTER.

MY MOM'S FIFTH PREGNANCY WAS REALLY HARD FOR HER, SHE SPENT A LOT OF TIME IN THE HOSPITAL OVERNIGHT.

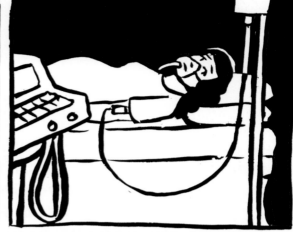

SHE ALSO HAD TO DO A TEMPORARY CAREER CHANGE FROM A CHILDCARE PROVIDER

TO A NANNY.

BUT EVENTUALLY MY SISTER MINNOW WAS BORN!

YAY!

YOU KNOW, SOMETIMES I THINK ABOUT WHAT MIGHT HAVE HAPPENED IF MY MOM HADN'T TERMINATED HER FIRST PREGNANCY. SHE AND MY DAD WOULD PROBABLY STILL LIVE UP ON CAPITOL HILL WITH THE WOULD-BE BABY, WHO'D BE SIX MONTHS OLDER THAN ME. IF THE FETUS WAS BORN A BOY THEN HIS NAME WOULD PROBABLY BE BRUNO OR SAYLER OR ONE OF THE OTHER NAMES MY PARENTS WOULD'VE NAMED ME IF I WERE ASSIGNED MALE AT BIRTH. IF IT WERE A GIRL HER NAME PROBABLY WOULD HAVE BEEN BEEZUS. SO SHE'D BE ME, BUT NOT REALLY. WOULD SHE HAVE ANY YOUNGER SIBLINGS? WOULD SHE BE ANYTHING LIKE ME? I NEVER REALLY THINK ABOUT THE TWO BABIES THAT MY MOM MISCARRIED BECAUSE I HAVE MY SISTER, SO I JUST ALWAYS ASSUMED THAT IT WAS ALL MEANT TO BE. IT'S WEIRD TO THINK ABOUT.

CHAPTER 4:

BLOOD, BATH, AND BEYOND

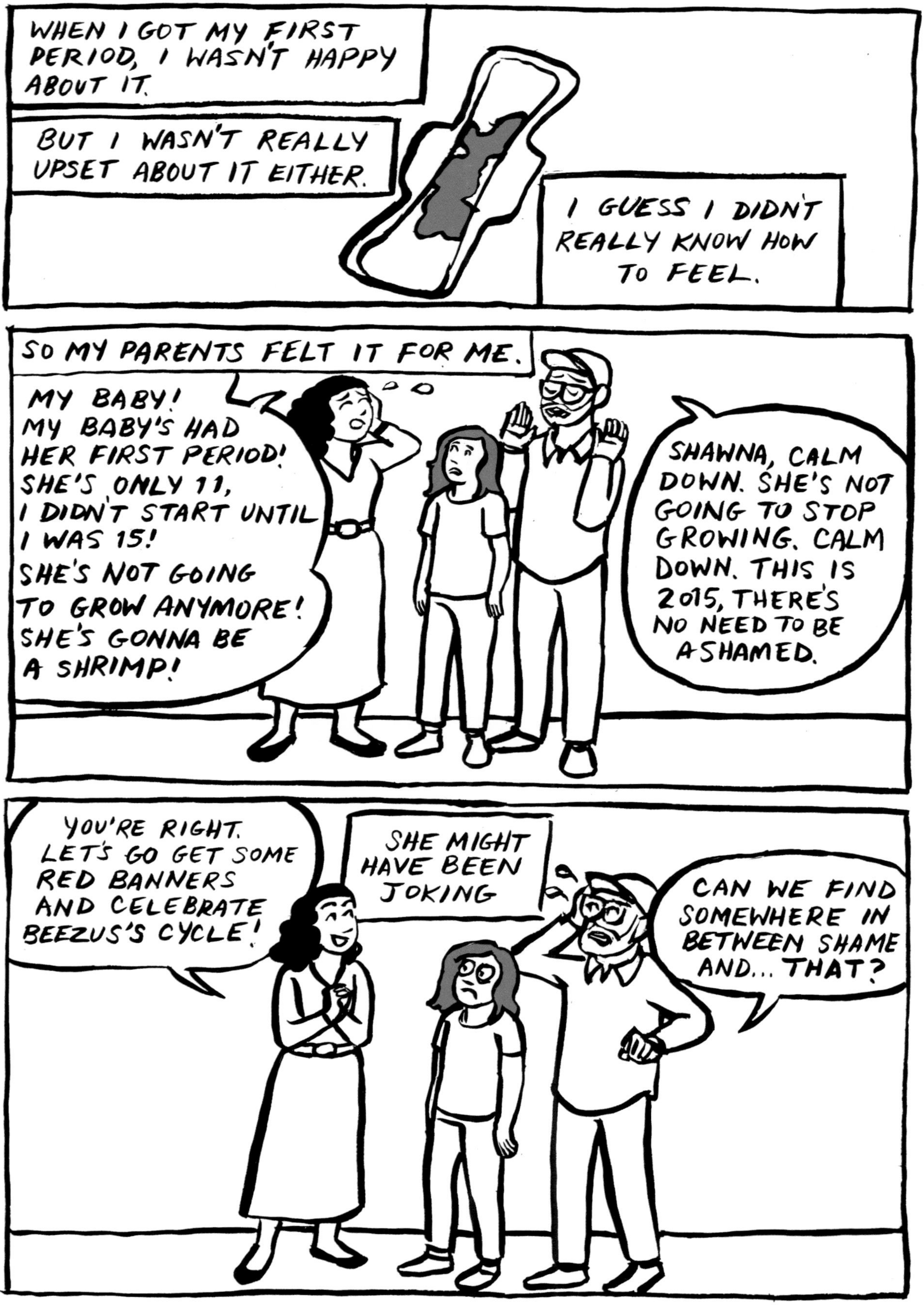

WHEN I GOT MY FIRST PERIOD, I WASN'T HAPPY ABOUT IT.
BUT I WASN'T REALLY UPSET ABOUT IT EITHER.
I GUESS I DIDN'T REALLY KNOW HOW TO FEEL.
SO MY PARENTS FELT IT FOR ME.
MY BABY! MY BABY'S HAD HER FIRST PERIOD! SHE'S ONLY 11, I DIDN'T START UNTIL I WAS 15! SHE'S NOT GOING TO GROW ANYMORE! SHE'S GONNA BE A SHRIMP!
SHAWNA, CALM DOWN. SHE'S NOT GOING TO STOP GROWING. CALM DOWN. THIS IS 2015, THERE'S NO NEED TO BE ASHAMED.
YOU'RE RIGHT. LET'S GO GET SOME RED BANNERS AND CELEBRATE BEEZUS'S CYCLE!
SHE MIGHT HAVE BEEN JOKING
CAN WE FIND SOMEWHERE IN BETWEEN SHAME AND... THAT?

MAYBE THE REASON WHY I DIDN'T KNOW WHAT TO FEEL WAS BECAUSE NO ONE EXCEPT MY MOTHER HAD EVER PREPARED ME FOR IT. I HAD NO PERSPECTIVE OTHER THAN HERS, AND HERS WASN'T REALLY THE TYPICAL EXPERIENCE. AFTER ALL SHE HAD STARTED AT 15, WHICH IS OLDER THAN MOST. AND AT THIS POINT IN MY LIFE I HAD SEEN NO MEDIA DEPICTING PERIODS. AS A KID I WOULD WATCH A LOT OF OLD-SCHOOL TV - 'FULL HOUSE,' 'BOY MEETS WORLD,' 'SABRINA THE TEENAGE WITCH,' 'SCOOBY-DOO,' 'DUCKTALES,' 'BEWITCHED,' 'GILLIGAN'S ISLAND ' - AND SOMETHING THAT ALWAYS BAFFLED ME ABOUT THE FIRST ONE WAS THAT MENSTRUATION WAS NEVER ADDRESSED. I MEAN, BY THE LAST SEASON OF 'FULL HOUSE' DJ, STEPHANIE, AND AUNT BECKY WERE ALL LIVING TOGETHER AND PROBABLY ALL GETTING THEIR PERIODS, AND KIMMY DROPPED BY ALL THE TIME, BUT THERE WAS NEVER ANY TALK ABOUT PMS, TAMPONS, PADS, SYNCING UP, OR PERIODS. I'M GLAD THAT IN THIS DAY AND AGE MENSTRUATION IS LESS OF A TABOO SUBJECT. NOT TO SAY THAT THEY NEVER TALKED ABOUT PERIODS ON TV BACK THEN, BUT NOT AS LIBERALLY AS THEY DO TODAY. BUT STILL, WHY MUST THE FEMALE BODY BE SUCH A TABOO SUBJECT? EXCEPT FOR, OF COURSE, WHEN IT'S PLEASING FOR THE (PRESUMABLY MALE) VIEWER.

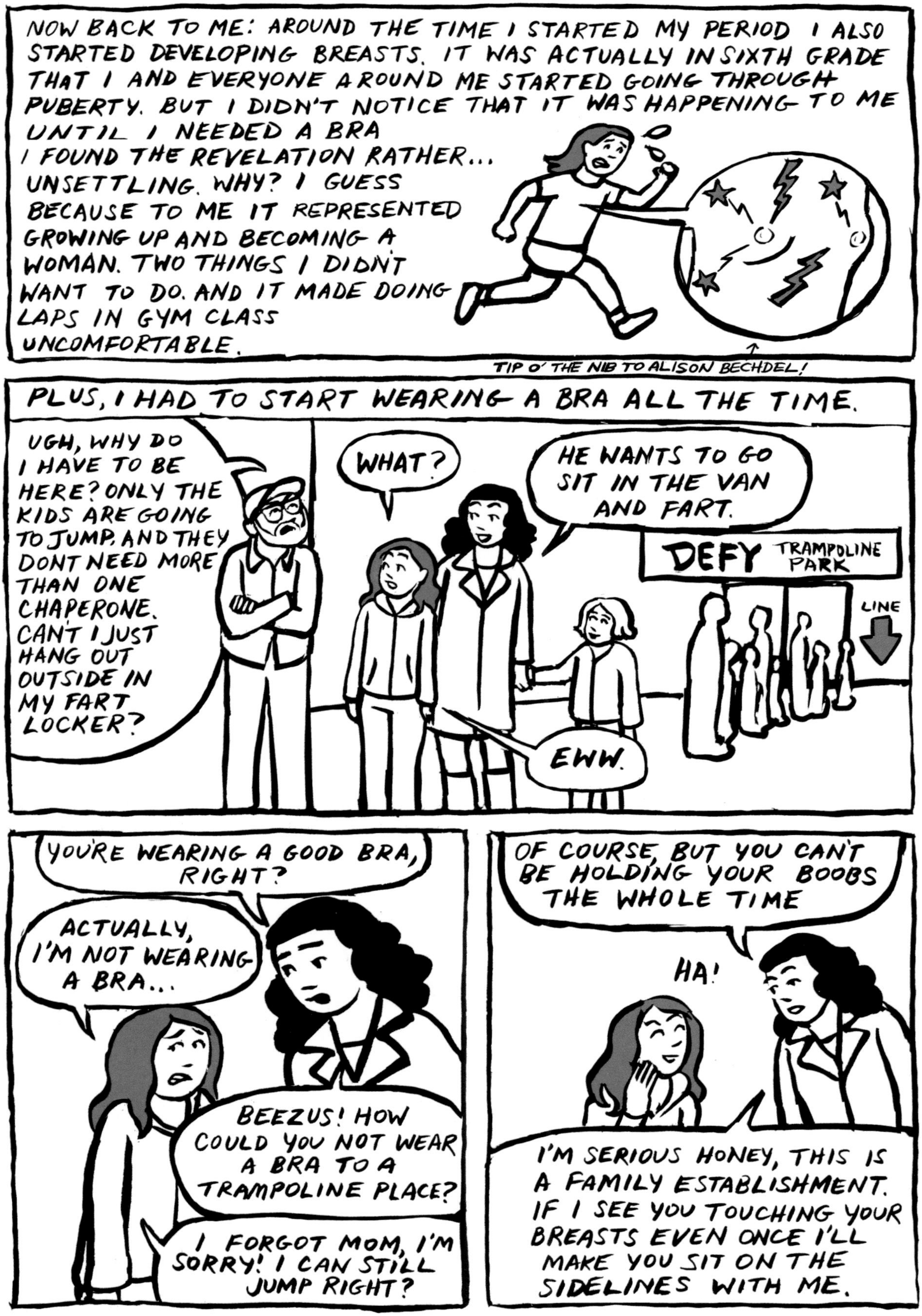
NOW BACK TO ME: AROUND THE TIME I STARTED MY PERIOD I ALSO STARTED DEVELOPING BREASTS. IT WAS ACTUALLY IN SIXTH GRADE THAT I AND EVERYONE AROUND ME STARTED GOING THROUGH PUBERTY. BUT I DIDN'T NOTICE THAT IT WAS HAPPENING TO ME UNTIL I NEEDED A BRA
I FOUND THE REVELATION RATHER... UNSETTLING. WHY? I GUESS BECAUSE TO ME IT REPRESENTED GROWING UP AND BECOMING A WOMAN. TWO THINGS I DIDN'T WANT TO DO. AND IT MADE DOING LAPS IN GYM CLASS UNCOMFORTABLE.
TIP O' THE NIB TO ALISON BECHDEL!
PLUS, I HAD TO START WEARING A BRA ALL THE TIME.
UGH, WHY DO I HAVE TO BE HERE? ONLY THE KIDS ARE GOING TO JUMP, AND THEY DONT NEED MORE THAN ONE CHAPERONE. CAN'T I JUST HANG OUT OUTSIDE IN MY FART LOCKER?
WHAT?
HE WANTS TO GO SIT IN THE VAN AND FART.
DEFY TRAMPOLINE PARK
LINE
EWW.
YOU'RE WEARING A GOOD BRA, RIGHT?
ACTUALLY, I'M NOT WEARING A BRA...
BEEZUS! HOW COULD YOU NOT WEAR A BRA TO A TRAMPOLINE PLACE?
I FORGOT MOM, I'M SORRY! I CAN STILL JUMP RIGHT?
OF COURSE, BUT YOU CAN'T BE HOLDING YOUR BOOBS THE WHOLE TIME
HA!
I'M SERIOUS HONEY, THIS IS A FAMILY ESTABLISHMENT. IF I SEE YOU TOUCHING YOUR BREASTS EVEN ONCE I'LL MAKE YOU SIT ON THE SIDELINES WITH ME.

CHAPTER 5:

YOUR MOTHER AND MINE

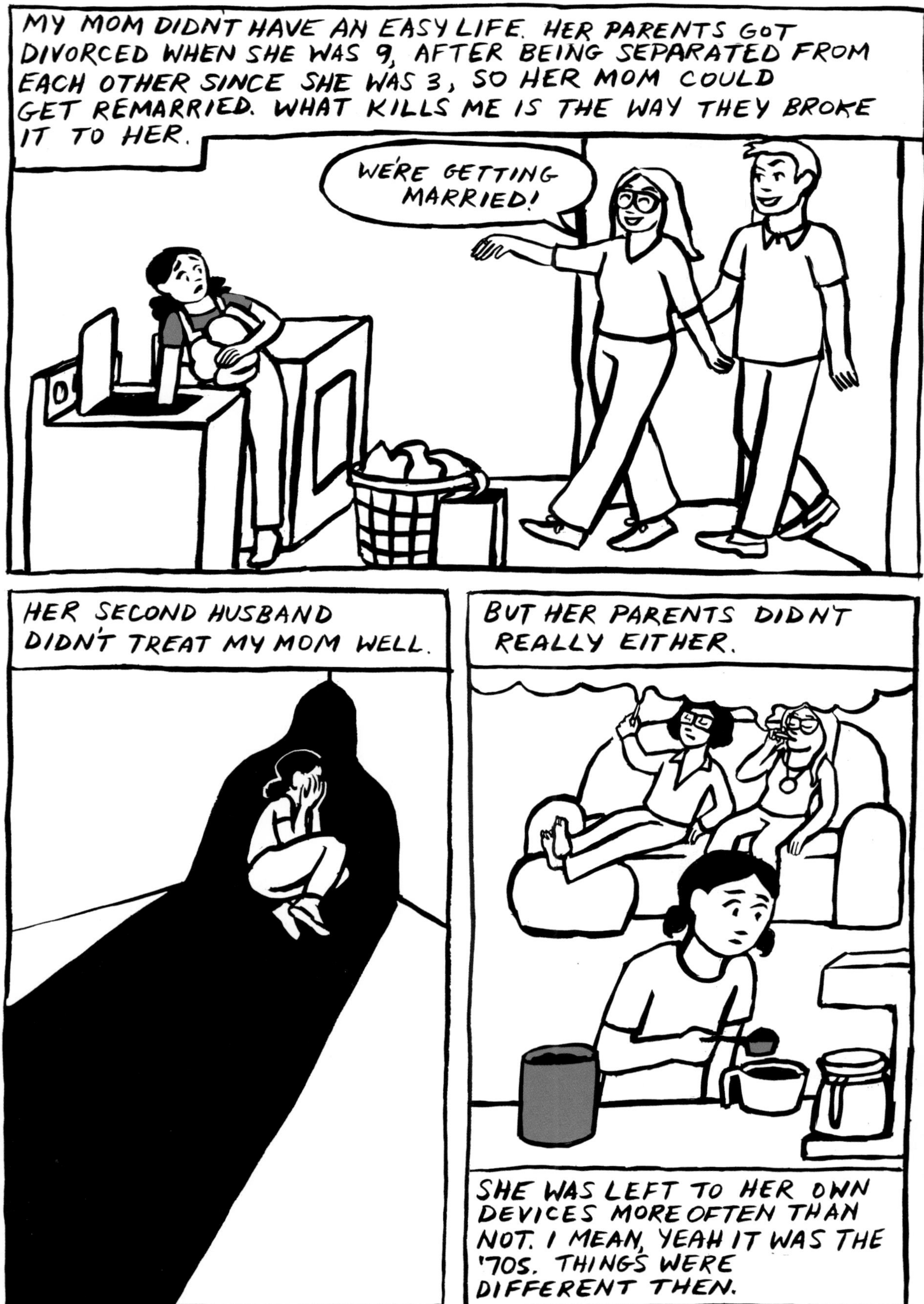
MY MOM DIDN'T HAVE AN EASY LIFE. HER PARENTS GOT DIVORCED WHEN SHE WAS 9, AFTER BEING SEPARATED FROM EACH OTHER SINCE SHE WAS 3, SO HER MOM COULD GET REMARRIED. WHAT KILLS ME IS THE WAY THEY BROKE IT TO HER.
WE'RE GETTING MARRIED!
HER SECOND HUSBAND DIDN'T TREAT MY MOM WELL.
BUT HER PARENTS DIDN'T REALLY EITHER.
SHE WAS LEFT TO HER OWN DEVICES MORE OFTEN THAN NOT. I MEAN, YEAH IT WAS THE '70S. THINGS WERE DIFFERENT THEN.

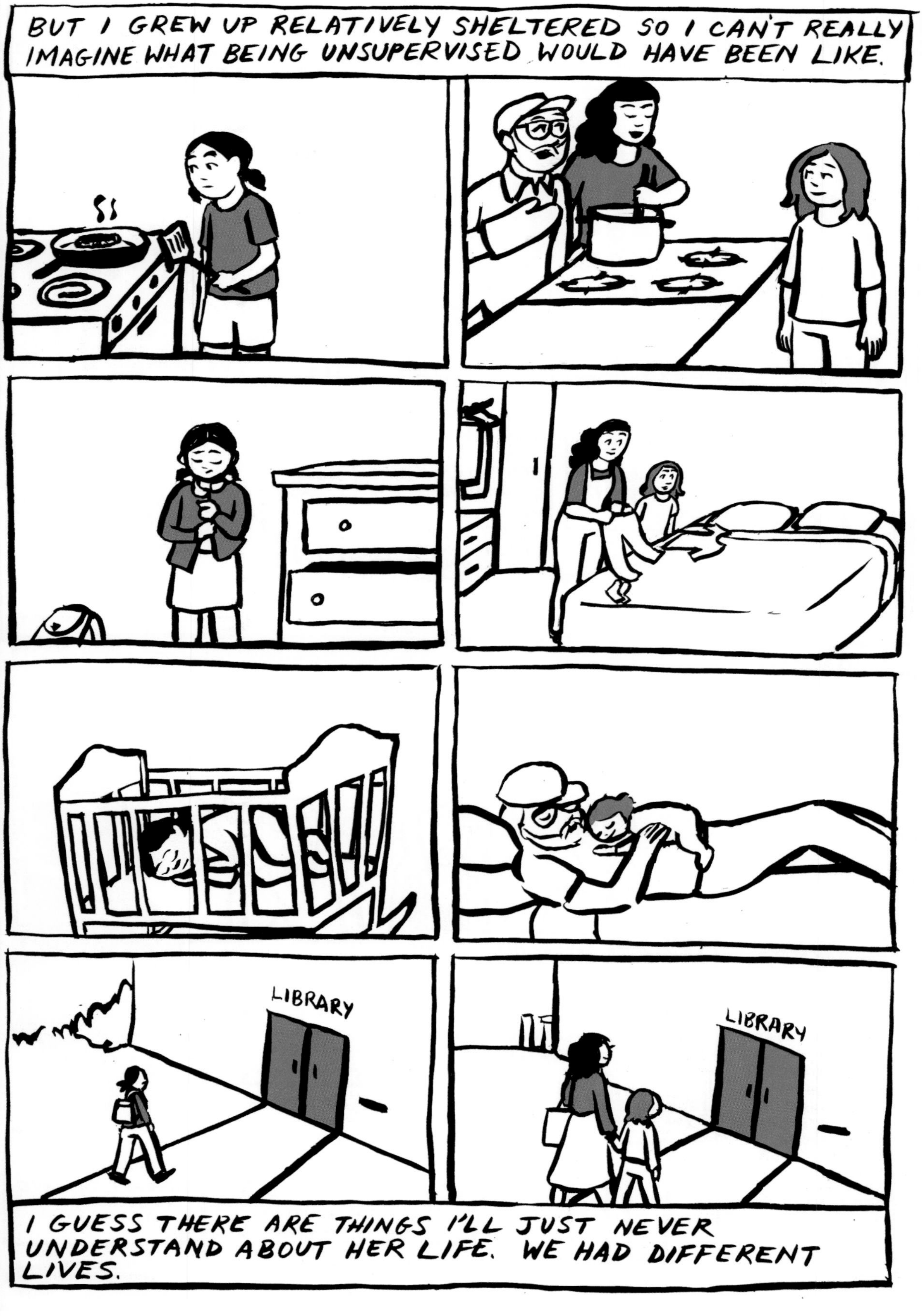
BUT I GREW UP RELATIVELY SHELTERED SO I CAN'T REALLY IMAGINE WHAT BEING UNSUPERVISED WOULD HAVE BEEN LIKE.
LIBRARY
LIBRARY
I GUESS THERE ARE THINGS I'LL JUST NEVER UNDERSTAND ABOUT HER LIFE. WE HAD DIFFERENT LIVES.

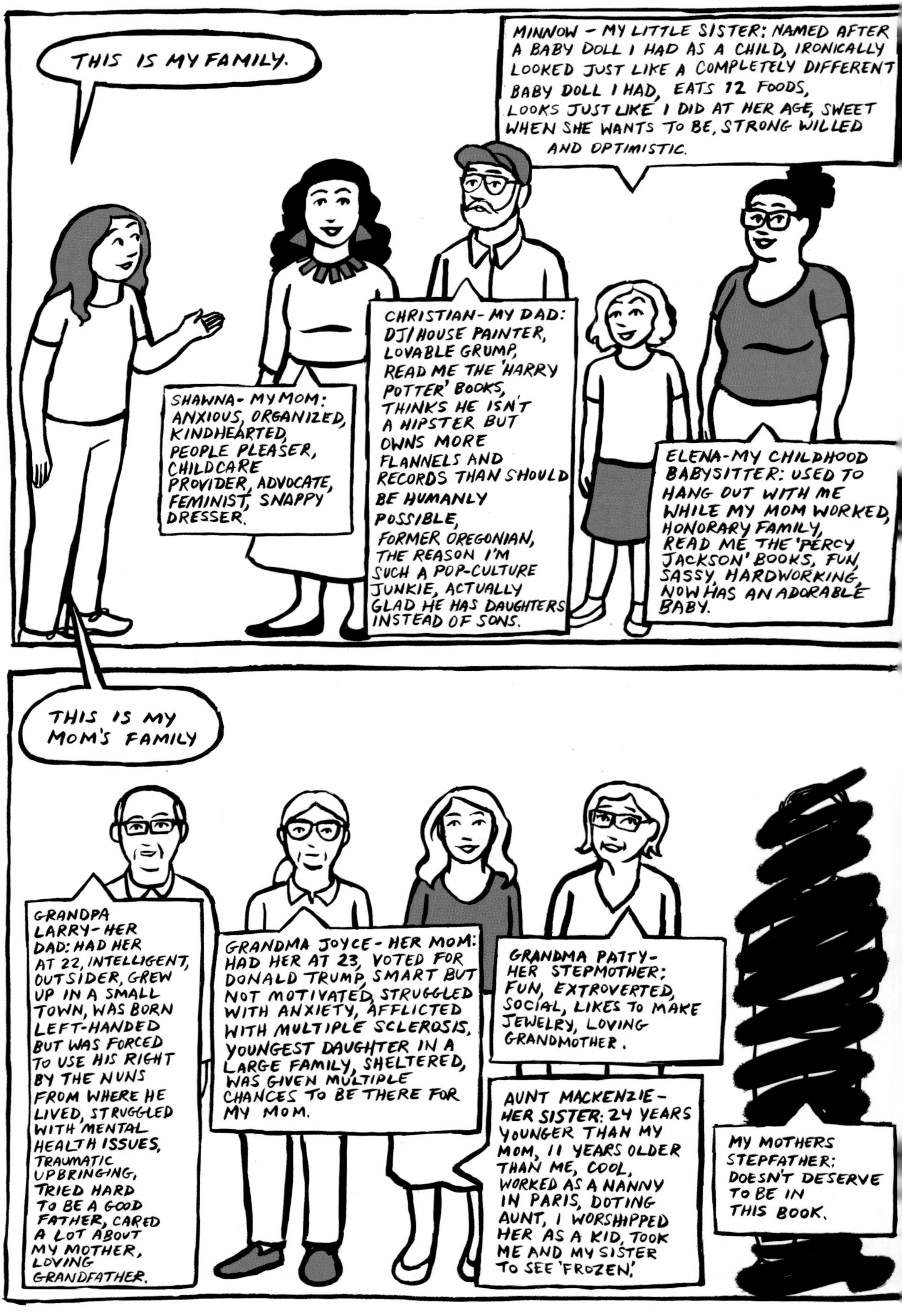
THIS IS MY FAMILY.
MINNOW - MY LITTLE SISTER: NAMED AFTER A BABY DOLL I HAD AS A CHILD, IRONICALLY LOOKED JUST LIKE A COMPLETELY DIFFERENT BABY DOLL I HAD, EATS 12 FOODS, LOOKS JUST LIKE I DID AT HER AGE, SWEET WHEN SHE WANTS TO BE, STRONG WILLED AND OPTIMISTIC.
SHAWNA- MY MOM: ANXIOUS, ORGANIZED, KINDHEARTED, PEOPLE PLEASER, CHILDCARE PROVIDER, ADVOCATE, FEMINIST, SNAPPY DRESSER.
CHRISTIAN- MY DAD: DJ/HOUSE PAINTER, LOVABLE GRUMP, READ ME THE 'HARRY POTTER' BOOKS, THINKS HE ISN'T A HIPSTER BUT OWNS MORE FLANNELS AND RECORDS THAN SHOULD BE HUMANLY POSSIBLE, FORMER OREGONIAN, THE REASON I'M SUCH A POP-CULTURE JUNKIE, ACTUALLY GLAD HE HAS DAUGHTERS INSTEAD OF SONS.
ELENA-MY CHILDHOOD BABYSITTER: USED TO HANG OUT WITH ME WHILE MY MOM WORKED, HONORARY FAMILY, READ ME THE 'PERCY JACKSON' BOOKS, FUN, SASSY, HARDWORKING, NOW HAS AN ADORABLE BABY.
THIS IS MY MOM'S FAMILY
GRANDPA LARRY- HER DAD: HAD HER AT 22, INTELLIGENT, OUTSIDER, GREW UP IN A SMALL TOWN, WAS BORN LEFT-HANDED BUT WAS FORCED TO USE HIS RIGHT BY THE NUNS FROM WHERE HE LIVED, STRUGGLED WITH MENTAL HEALTH ISSUES, TRAUMATIC UPBRINGING, TRIED HARD TO BE A GOOD FATHER, CARED A LOT ABOUT MY MOTHER, LOVING GRANDFATHER.
GRANDMA JOYCE - HER MOM: HAD HER AT 23, VOTED FOR DONALD TRUMP, SMART BUT NOT MOTIVATED, STRUGGLED WITH ANXIETY, AFFLICTED WITH MULTIPLE SCLEROSIS, YOUNGEST DAUGHTER IN A LARGE FAMILY, SHELTERED, WAS GIVEN MULTIPLE CHANCES TO BE THERE FOR MY MOM.
GRANDMA PATTY- HER STEPMOTHER: FUN, EXTROVERTED, SOCIAL, LIKES TO MAKE JEWELRY, LOVING GRANDMOTHER.
AUNT MACKENZIE- HER SISTER: 24 YEARS YOUNGER THAN MY MOM, 11 YEARS OLDER THAN ME, COOL, WORKED AS A NANNY IN PARIS, DOTING AUNT, I WORSHIPPED HER AS A KID, TOOK ME AND MY SISTER TO SEE 'FROZEN.'
MY MOTHERS STEPFATHER: DOESN'T DESERVE TO BE IN THIS BOOK.

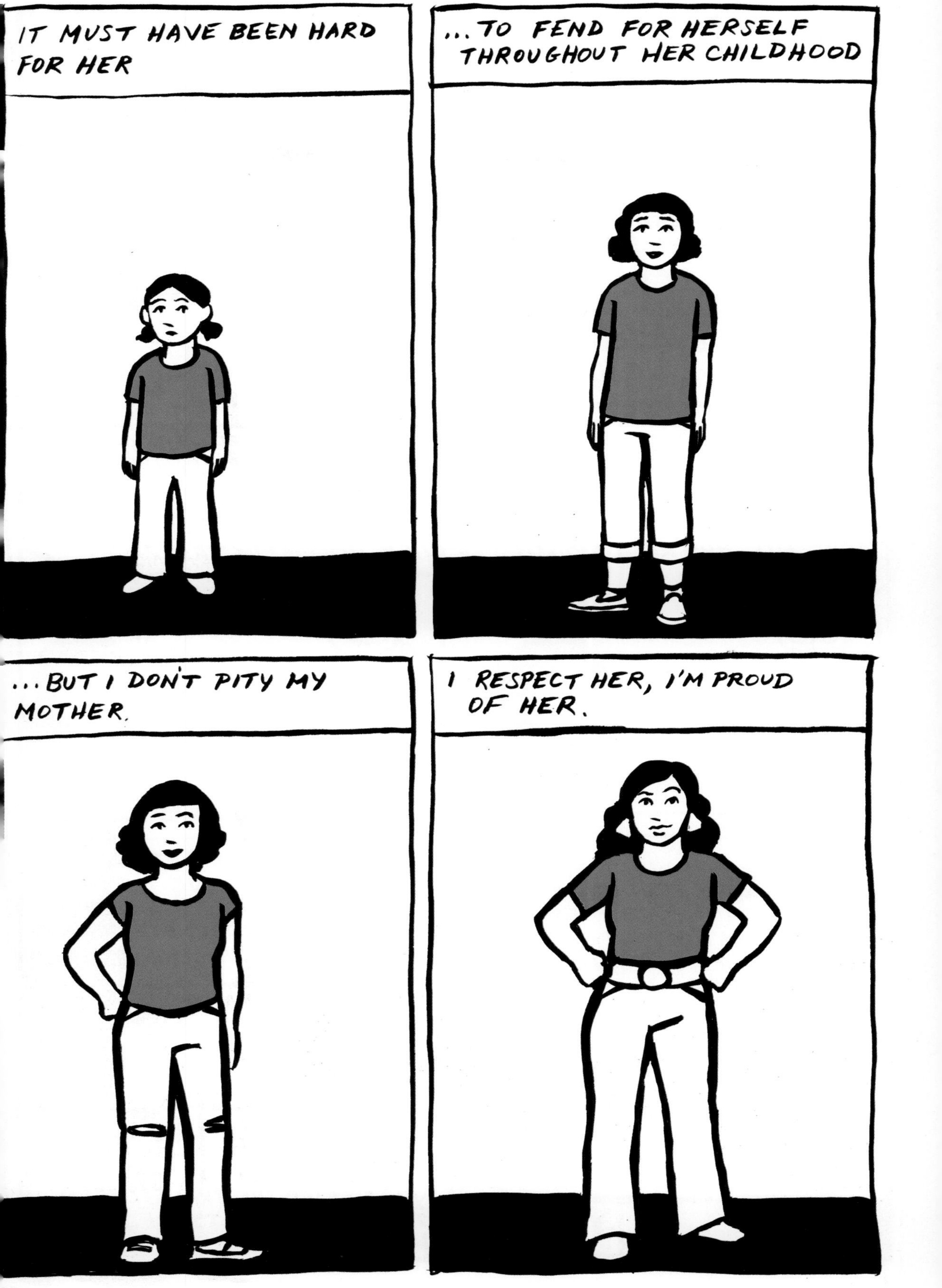
IT MUST HAVE BEEN HARD FOR HER
...TO FEND FOR HERSELF THROUGHOUT HER CHILDHOOD
...BUT I DON'T PITY MY MOTHER.
I RESPECT HER, I'M PROUD OF HER.

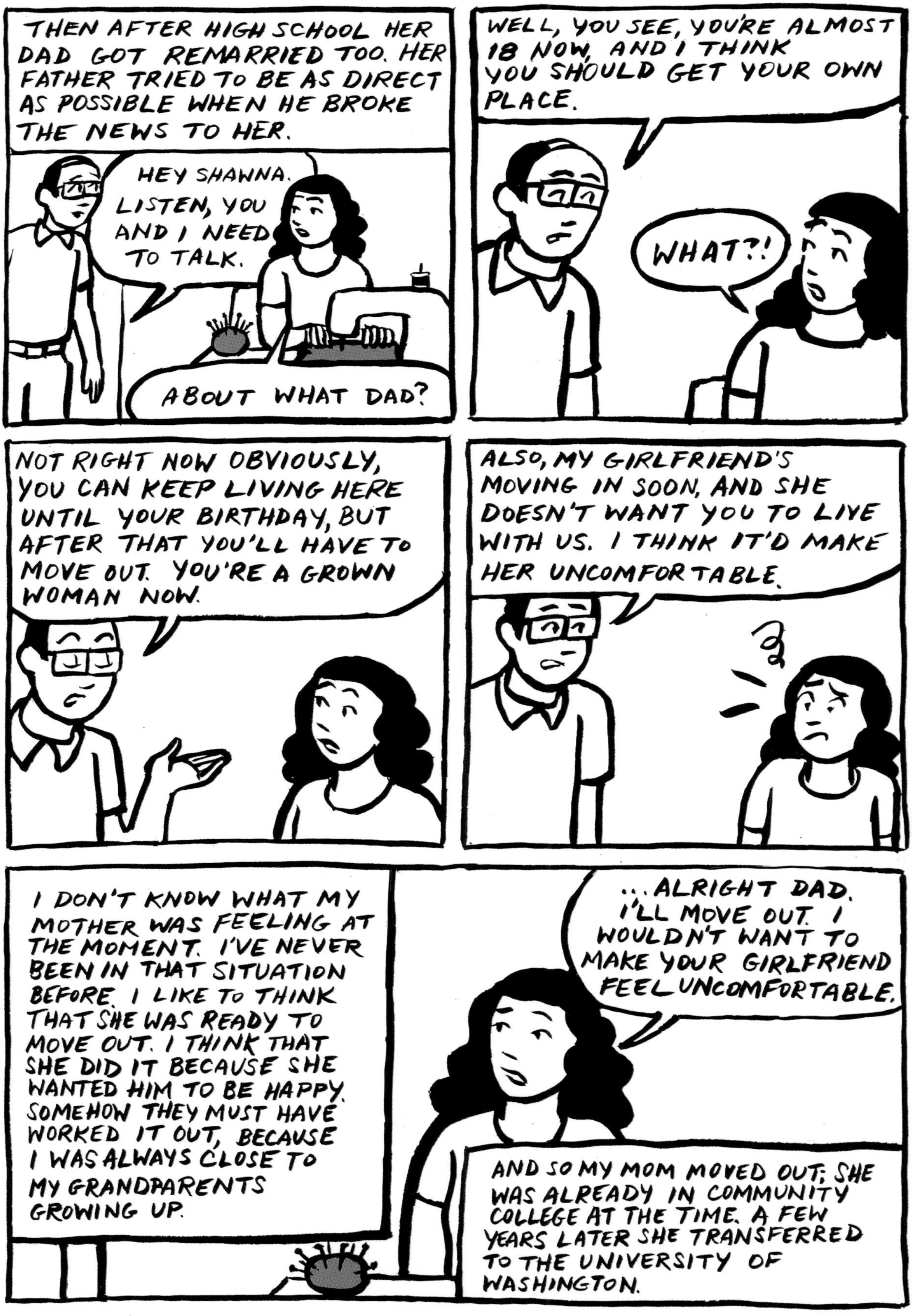
THEN AFTER HIGH SCHOOL HER DAD GOT REMARRIED TOO. HER FATHER TRIED TO BE AS DIRECT AS POSSIBLE WHEN HE BROKE THE NEWS TO HER.
HEY SHAWNA. LISTEN, YOU AND I NEED TO TALK.
ABOUT WHAT DAD?
WELL, YOU SEE, YOU'RE ALMOST 18 NOW, AND I THINK YOU SHOULD GET YOUR OWN PLACE.
WHAT?!
NOT RIGHT NOW OBVIOUSLY, YOU CAN KEEP LIVING HERE UNTIL YOUR BIRTHDAY, BUT AFTER THAT YOU'LL HAVE TO MOVE OUT. YOU'RE A GROWN WOMAN NOW.
ALSO, MY GIRLFRIEND'S MOVING IN SOON, AND SHE DOESN'T WANT YOU TO LIVE WITH US. I THINK IT'D MAKE HER UNCOMFORTABLE.
I DON'T KNOW WHAT MY MOTHER WAS FEELING AT THE MOMENT. I'VE NEVER BEEN IN THAT SITUATION BEFORE. I LIKE TO THINK THAT SHE WAS READY TO MOVE OUT. I THINK THAT SHE DID IT BECAUSE SHE WANTED HIM TO BE HAPPY. SOMEHOW THEY MUST HAVE WORKED IT OUT, BECAUSE I WAS ALWAYS CLOSE TO MY GRANDPARENTS GROWING UP.
...ALRIGHT DAD. I'LL MOVE OUT. I WOULDN'T WANT TO MAKE YOUR GIRLFRIEND FEEL UNCOMFORTABLE.
AND SO MY MOM MOVED OUT; SHE WAS ALREADY IN COMMUNITY COLLEGE AT THE TIME. A FEW YEARS LATER SHE TRANSFERRED TO THE UNIVERSITY OF WASHINGTON.

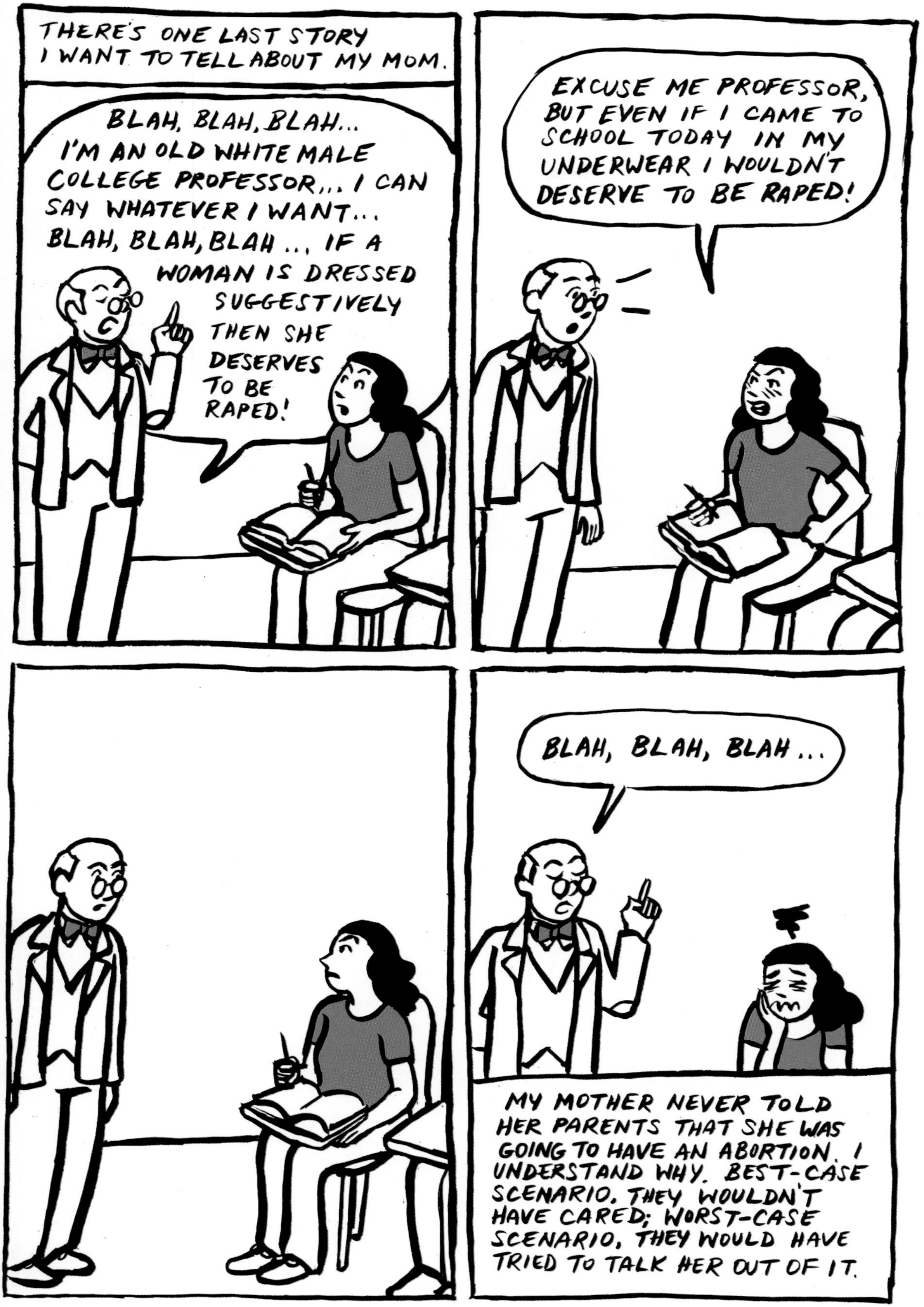
THERE'S ONE LAST STORY I WANT TO TELL ABOUT MY MOM.
BLAH, BLAH, BLAH... I'M AN OLD WHITE MALE COLLEGE PROFESSOR... I CAN SAY WHATEVER I WANT... BLAH, BLAH, BLAH..., IF A WOMAN IS DRESSED SUGGESTIVELY THEN SHE DESERVES TO BE RAPED!
EXCUSE ME PROFESSOR, BUT EVEN IF I CAME TO SCHOOL TODAY IN MY UNDERWEAR I WOULDN'T DESERVE TO BE RAPED!
BLAH, BLAH, BLAH...
MY MOTHER NEVER TOLD HER PARENTS THAT SHE WAS GOING TO HAVE AN ABORTION. I UNDERSTAND WHY. BEST-CASE SCENARIO, THEY WOULDN'T HAVE CARED; WORST-CASE SCENARIO, THEY WOULD HAVE TRIED TO TALK HER OUT OF IT.

CHAPTER 6:

GROWING UP GAY

SOMETHING THAT I HAVE NEGLECTED TO MENTION THUS FAR IS THAT I AM A LESBIAN. Y'KNOW IT'S FUNNY, I TRIED WATCHING THE TV SHOW 'THE L WORD' A COUPLE TIMES BUT I WASN'T INTO IT. I THINK THAT I FIRST REALIZED WHEN I WAS ABOUT 8, BUT I DIDN'T KNOW FOR SURE UNTIL I WAS 11. THAT'S WHEN I HAD MY FIRST REAL CRUSH. HER NAME WAS DYLIN, DYLIN PLEASANT. THERE ACTUALLY WERE TWO OTHER DYLANS IN MY GRADE, DYLAN BLACK AND DILLON BAYER. WE ALL CALLED THEM GIRL DYLAN AND BOY DILLON BECAUSE THEY BOTH HAD LAST NAMES THAT START WITH A B.

GIRL DYLAN WAS AN ASSHOLE,

AND BOY DILLON AND I WERE NEVER THAT CLOSE,

BUT MY DYLIN WAS PERFECT.

SHE WAS COOL AND FUN AND EVERYONE REALLY LIKED HER A LOT. I REMEMBER WHEN I TOLD HER THAT I LIKED HER SHE HAD HER FRIEND, LET'S CALL HER KRISTEN, REJECT ME FOR HER.

WELL, DYLIN DOESN'T WANT TO HURT YOUR FEELINGS BUT, UH, YOU'RE NOT REALLY HER TYPE.

IT'S FINE. I GET IT.

AND SHE WANTS YOU TO KNOW THAT THIS DOESN'T MEAN YOU CAN'T BE FRIENDS.

NOW SHE MAY HAVE LET ME DOWN EASY, BUT OBVIOUSLY
I WOULD HAVE PREFERRED IT IF DYLIN HAD TOLD ME HERSELF.
WEIRDLY ENOUGH, WHEN I CAME OUT NO ONE REALLY CARED
THAT MUCH. WHICH WAS SURPRISING BECAUSE I HAD BEEN
PICKED ON A LOT DURING ELEMENTARY AND MIDDLE SCHOOL.
FOR A WHILE IN THIRD GRADE MY CLASSMATES EVEN INVENTED
SOMETHING CALLED "THE BEEZUS TOUCH" - THIS WAS BACK WHEN
'DIARY OF A WIMPY KID' WAS STILL POPULAR - AND REFUSED
TO TOUCH ME UNTIL MY TEACHER STEPPED IN. BUT AT LEAST
MY CLASSMATES WEREN'T HOMOPHOBIC.

I THINK THAT PART OF THE REASON WHY AT FIRST I WAS SO
UNSYMPATHETIC TO PEOPLE WHO HAD GOTTEN ABORTIONS
WAS BECAUSE I KNEW THAT I WOULD PROBABLY NEVER GET
PREGNANT BY ACCIDENT. IF I GOT PREGNANT IT WOULD BE
BECAUSE I WANTED TO. ALL OF THE LESBIANS WITH KIDS
THAT ME AND MY FAMILY KNEW HAD ADOPTED OR GOTTEN
ARTIFICIALLY INSEMINATED.

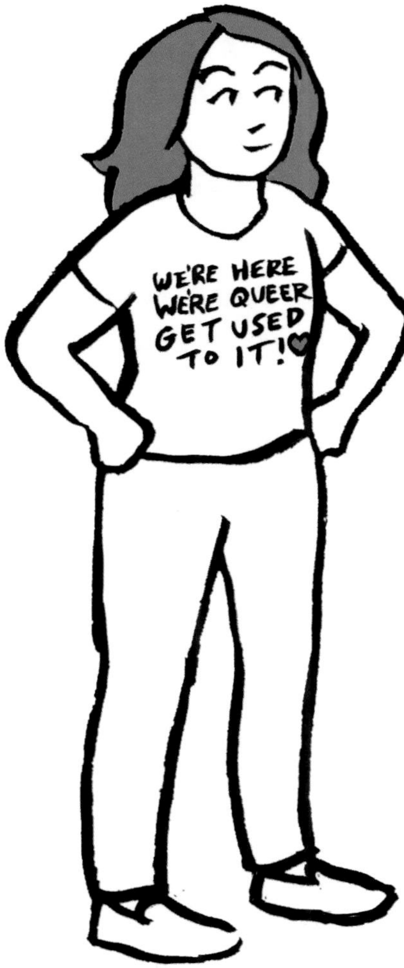
WE'RE HERE
WE'RE QUEER
GET USED
TO IT!

CHAPTER 7:

FIGHTING THE GOOD FIGHT

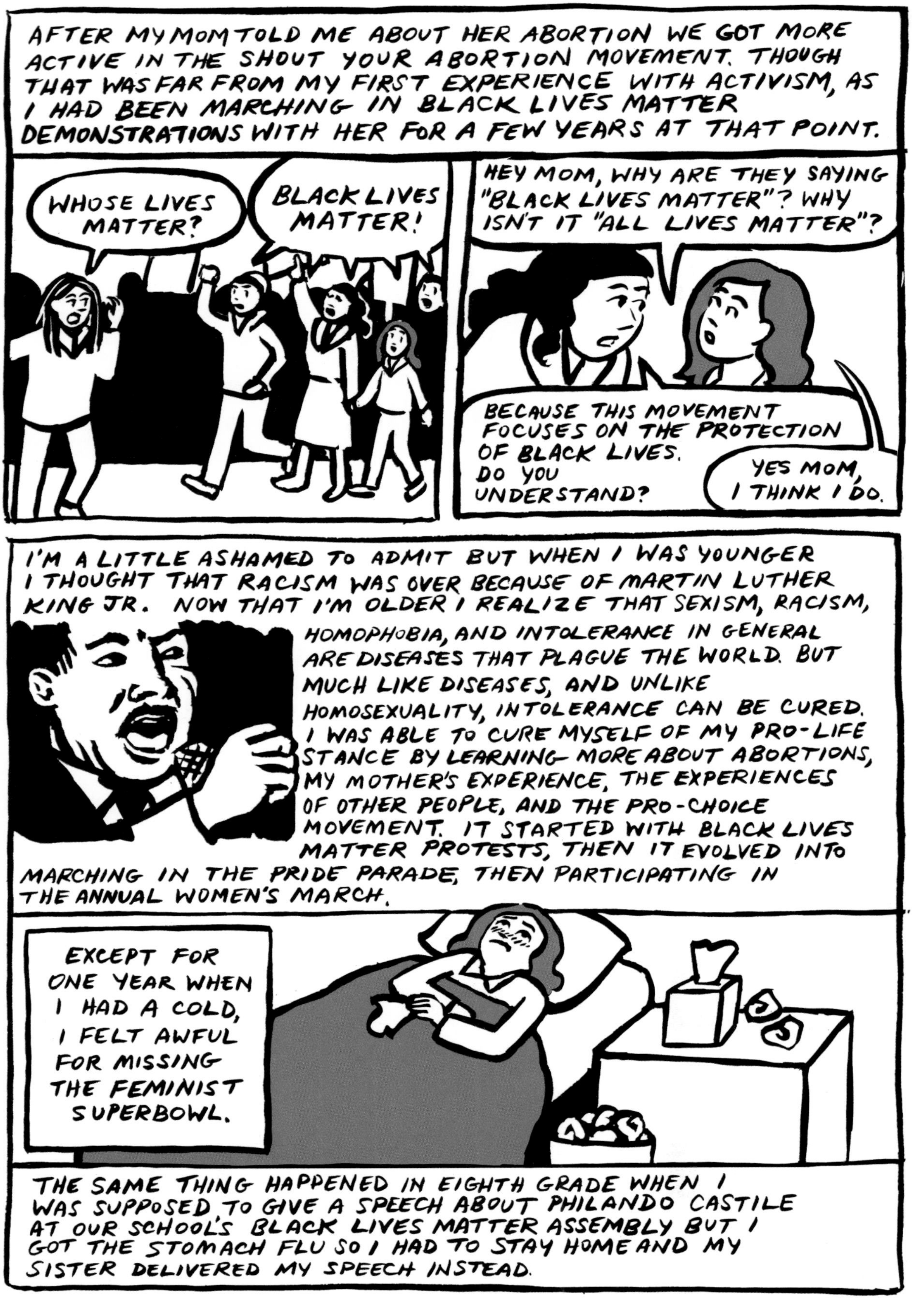
AFTER MY MOM TOLD ME ABOUT HER ABORTION WE GOT MORE ACTIVE IN THE SHOUT YOUR ABORTION MOVEMENT. THOUGH THAT WAS FAR FROM MY FIRST EXPERIENCE WITH ACTIVISM, AS I HAD BEEN MARCHING IN BLACK LIVES MATTER DEMONSTRATIONS WITH HER FOR A FEW YEARS AT THAT POINT.
WHOSE LIVES MATTER?
BLACK LIVES MATTER!
HEY MOM, WHY ARE THEY SAYING "BLACK LIVES MATTER"? WHY ISN'T IT "ALL LIVES MATTER"?
BECAUSE THIS MOVEMENT FOCUSES ON THE PROTECTION OF BLACK LIVES. DO YOU UNDERSTAND?
YES MOM, I THINK I DO.
I'M A LITTLE ASHAMED TO ADMIT BUT WHEN I WAS YOUNGER I THOUGHT THAT RACISM WAS OVER BECAUSE OF MARTIN LUTHER KING JR. NOW THAT I'M OLDER I REALIZE THAT SEXISM, RACISM, HOMOPHOBIA, AND INTOLERANCE IN GENERAL ARE DISEASES THAT PLAGUE THE WORLD. BUT MUCH LIKE DISEASES, AND UNLIKE HOMOSEXUALITY, INTOLERANCE CAN BE CURED. I WAS ABLE TO CURE MYSELF OF MY PRO-LIFE STANCE BY LEARNING MORE ABOUT ABORTIONS, MY MOTHER'S EXPERIENCE, THE EXPERIENCES OF OTHER PEOPLE, AND THE PRO-CHOICE MOVEMENT. IT STARTED WITH BLACK LIVES MATTER PROTESTS, THEN IT EVOLVED INTO MARCHING IN THE PRIDE PARADE, THEN PARTICIPATING IN THE ANNUAL WOMEN'S MARCH.
EXCEPT FOR ONE YEAR WHEN I HAD A COLD, I FELT AWFUL FOR MISSING THE FEMINIST SUPERBOWL.
THE SAME THING HAPPENED IN EIGHTH GRADE WHEN I WAS SUPPOSED TO GIVE A SPEECH ABOUT PHILANDO CASTILE AT OUR SCHOOL'S BLACK LIVES MATTER ASSEMBLY BUT I GOT THE STOMACH FLU SO I HAD TO STAY HOME AND MY SISTER DELIVERED MY SPEECH INSTEAD.

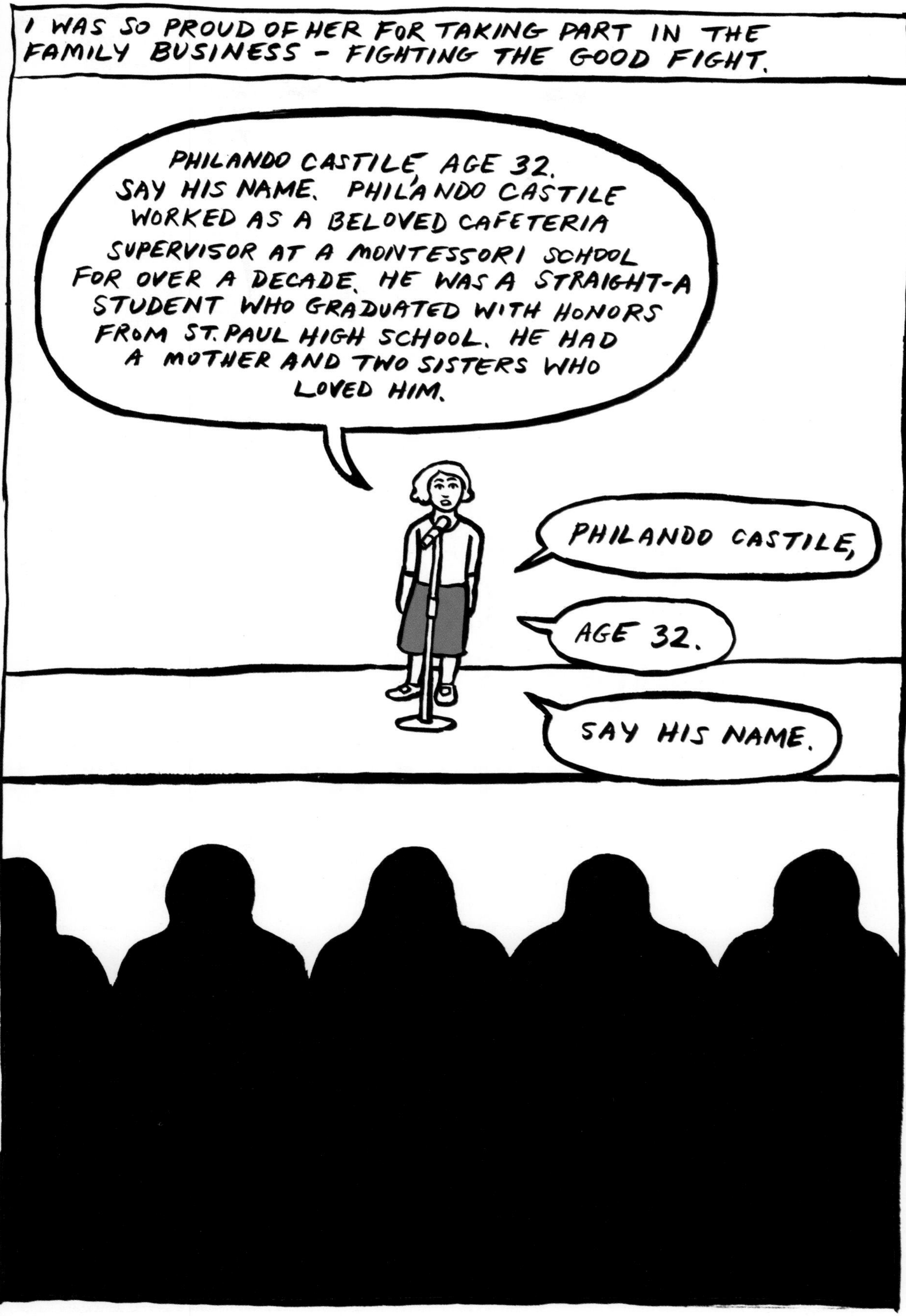
I WAS SO PROUD OF HER FOR TAKING PART IN THE FAMILY BUSINESS - FIGHTING THE GOOD FIGHT.
PHILANDO CASTILE, AGE 32. SAY HIS NAME. PHILANDO CASTILE WORKED AS A BELOVED CAFETERIA SUPERVISOR AT A MONTESSORI SCHOOL FOR OVER A DECADE. HE WAS A STRAIGHT-A STUDENT WHO GRADUATED WITH HONORS FROM ST. PAUL HIGH SCHOOL. HE HAD A MOTHER AND TWO SISTERS WHO LOVED HIM.
PHILANDO CASTILE,
AGE 32.
SAY HIS NAME.

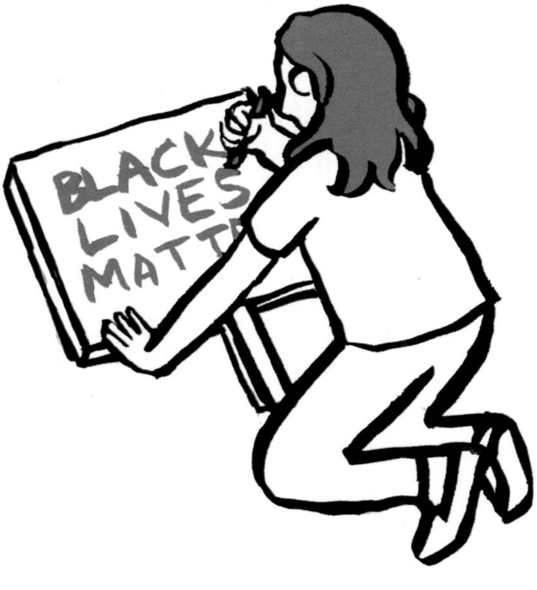
BLACK
LIVES
MATT

CHAPTER 8:

I'M DREAMING OF A RED CHRISTMAS

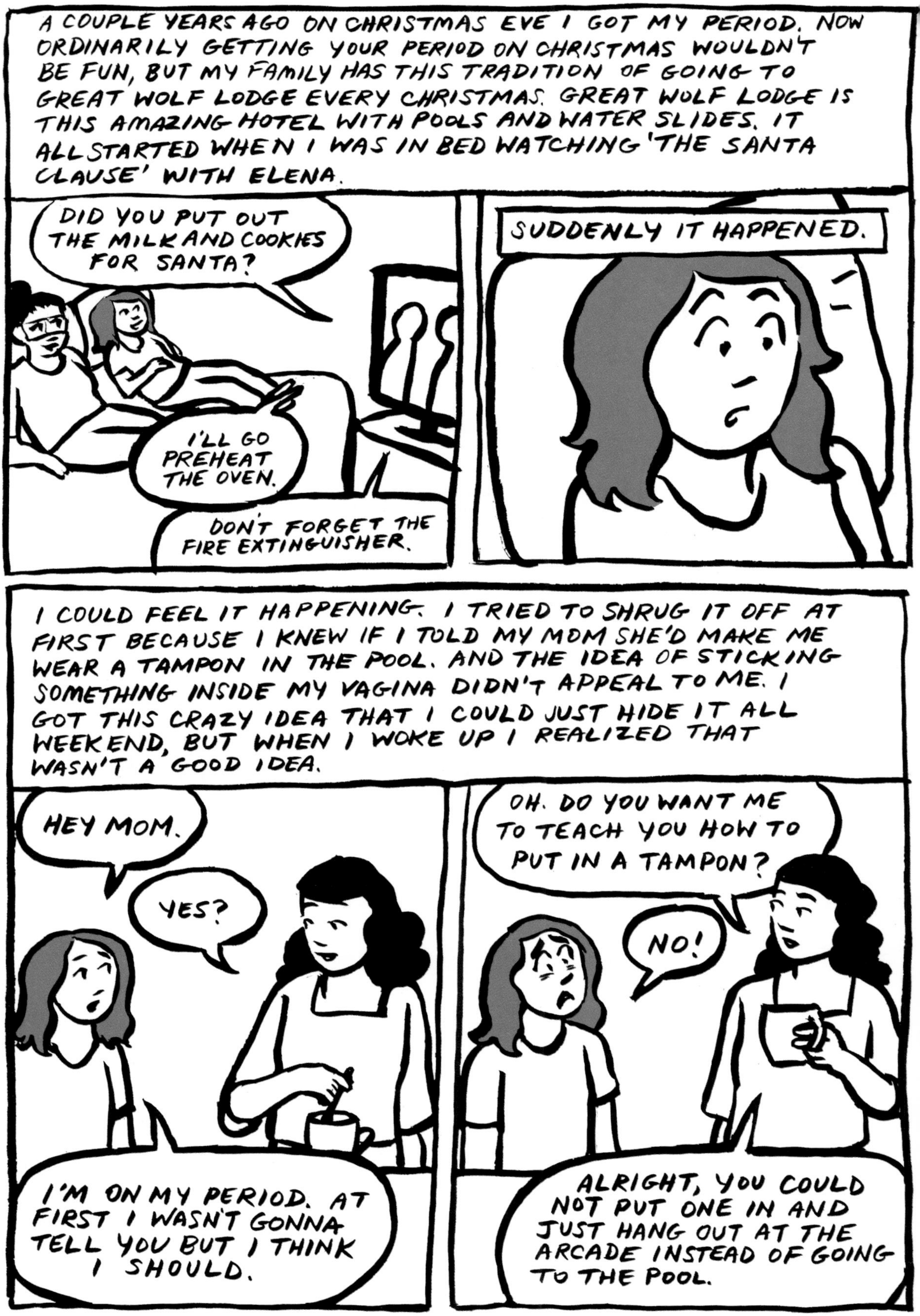
A COUPLE YEARS AGO ON CHRISTMAS EVE I GOT MY PERIOD. NOW ORDINARILY GETTING YOUR PERIOD ON CHRISTMAS WOULDN'T BE FUN, BUT MY FAMILY HAS THIS TRADITION OF GOING TO GREAT WOLF LODGE EVERY CHRISTMAS. GREAT WOLF LODGE IS THIS AMAZING HOTEL WITH POOLS AND WATER SLIDES. IT ALL STARTED WHEN I WAS IN BED WATCHING 'THE SANTA CLAUSE' WITH ELENA.
DID YOU PUT OUT THE MILK AND COOKIES FOR SANTA?
I'LL GO PREHEAT THE OVEN.
DON'T FORGET THE FIRE EXTINGUISHER.
SUDDENLY IT HAPPENED.
I COULD FEEL IT HAPPENING. I TRIED TO SHRUG IT OFF AT FIRST BECAUSE I KNEW IF I TOLD MY MOM SHE'D MAKE ME WEAR A TAMPON IN THE POOL. AND THE IDEA OF STICKING SOMETHING INSIDE MY VAGINA DIDN'T APPEAL TO ME. I GOT THIS CRAZY IDEA THAT I COULD JUST HIDE IT ALL WEEKEND, BUT WHEN I WOKE UP I REALIZED THAT WASN'T A GOOD IDEA.
HEY MOM.
YES?
I'M ON MY PERIOD. AT FIRST I WASN'T GONNA TELL YOU BUT I THINK I SHOULD.
OH. DO YOU WANT ME TO TEACH YOU HOW TO PUT IN A TAMPON?
NO!
ALRIGHT, YOU COULD NOT PUT ONE IN AND JUST HANG OUT AT THE ARCADE INSTEAD OF GOING TO THE POOL.

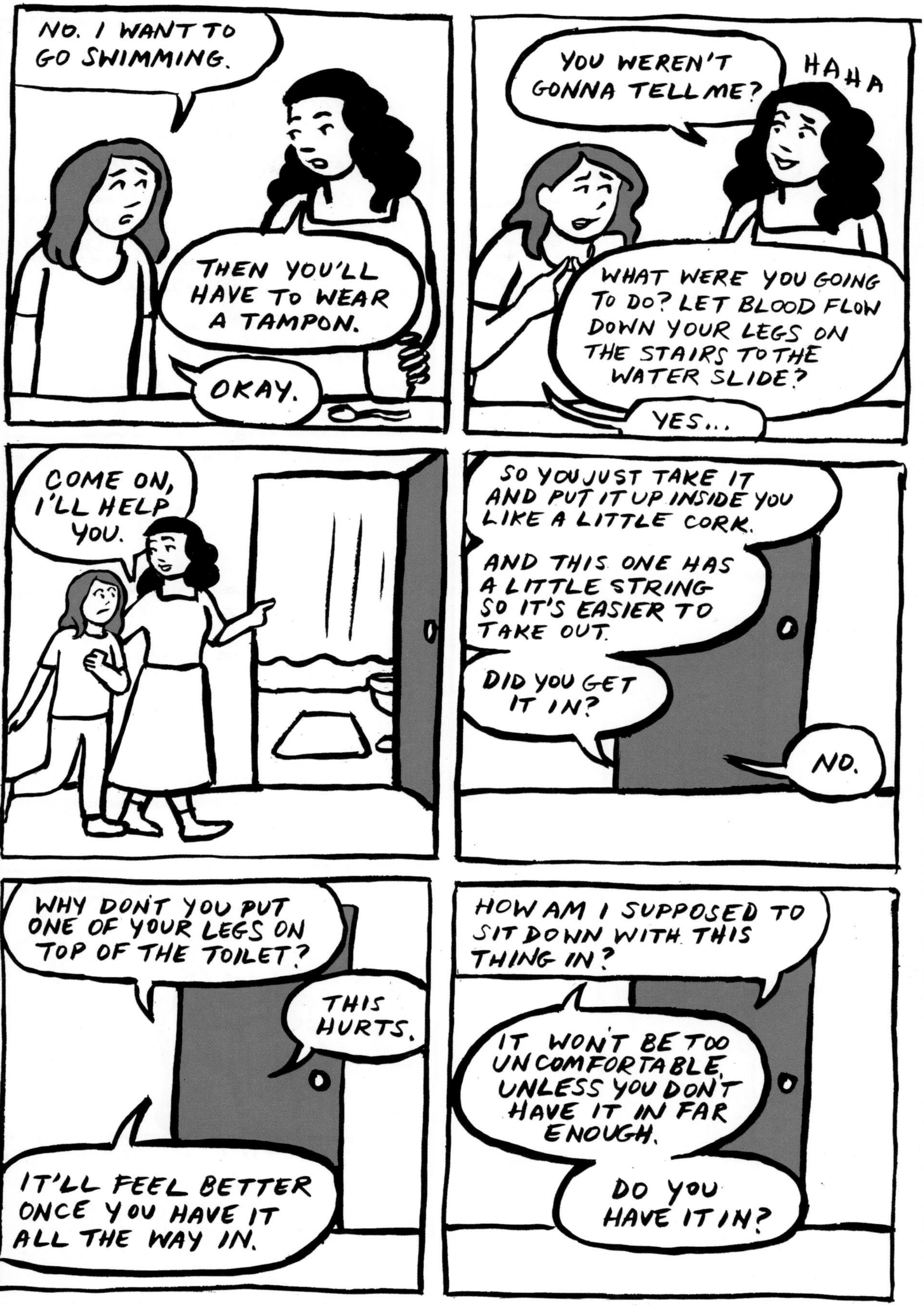
NO. I WANT TO GO SWIMMING.
THEN YOU'LL HAVE TO WEAR A TAMPON.
OKAY.
YOU WEREN'T GONNA TELL ME?
HAHA
WHAT WERE YOU GOING TO DO? LET BLOOD FLOW DOWN YOUR LEGS ON THE STAIRS TO THE WATER SLIDE?
YES...
COME ON, I'LL HELP YOU.
SO YOU JUST TAKE IT AND PUT IT UP INSIDE YOU LIKE A LITTLE CORK.
AND THIS ONE HAS A LITTLE STRING SO IT'S EASIER TO TAKE OUT.
DID YOU GET IT IN?
NO.
WHY DON'T YOU PUT ONE OF YOUR LEGS ON TOP OF THE TOILET?
THIS HURTS.
IT'LL FEEL BETTER ONCE YOU HAVE IT ALL THE WAY IN.
HOW AM I SUPPOSED TO SIT DOWN WITH THIS THING IN?
IT WON'T BE TOO UNCOMFORTABLE, UNLESS YOU DON'T HAVE IT IN FAR ENOUGH.
DO YOU HAVE IT IN?

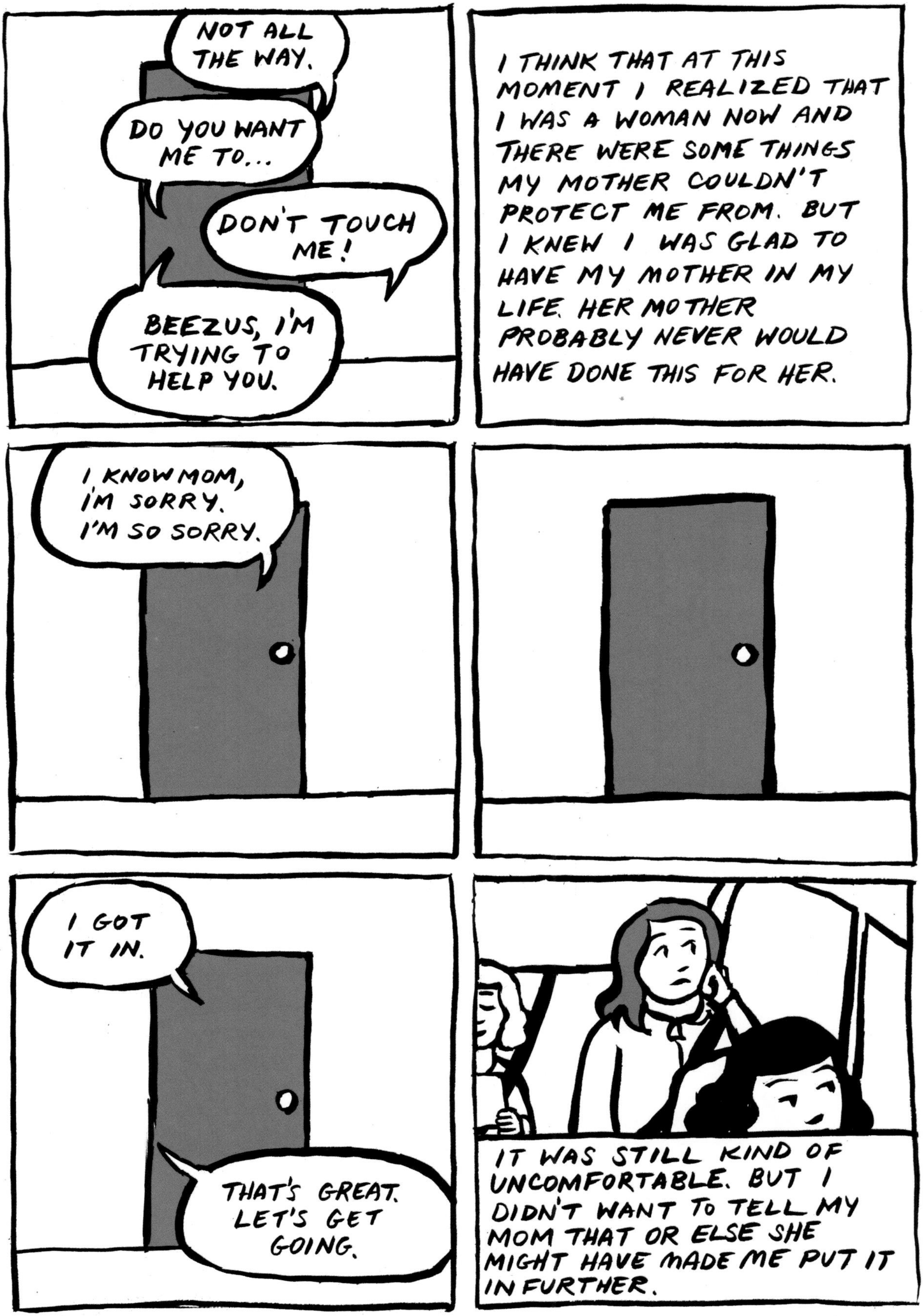
NOT ALL THE WAY.
DO YOU WANT ME TO...
DON'T TOUCH ME!
BEEZUS, I'M TRYING TO HELP YOU.
I THINK THAT AT THIS MOMENT I REALIZED THAT I WAS A WOMAN NOW AND THERE WERE SOME THINGS MY MOTHER COULDN'T PROTECT ME FROM. BUT I KNEW I WAS GLAD TO HAVE MY MOTHER IN MY LIFE. HER MOTHER PROBABLY NEVER WOULD HAVE DONE THIS FOR HER.
I KNOW MOM, I'M SORRY. I'M SO SORRY.
I GOT IT IN.
THAT'S GREAT. LET'S GET GOING.
IT WAS STILL KIND OF UNCOMFORTABLE. BUT I DIDN'T WANT TO TELL MY MOM THAT OR ELSE SHE MIGHT HAVE MADE ME PUT IT IN FURTHER.

CHAPTER 9:

SHOUT!

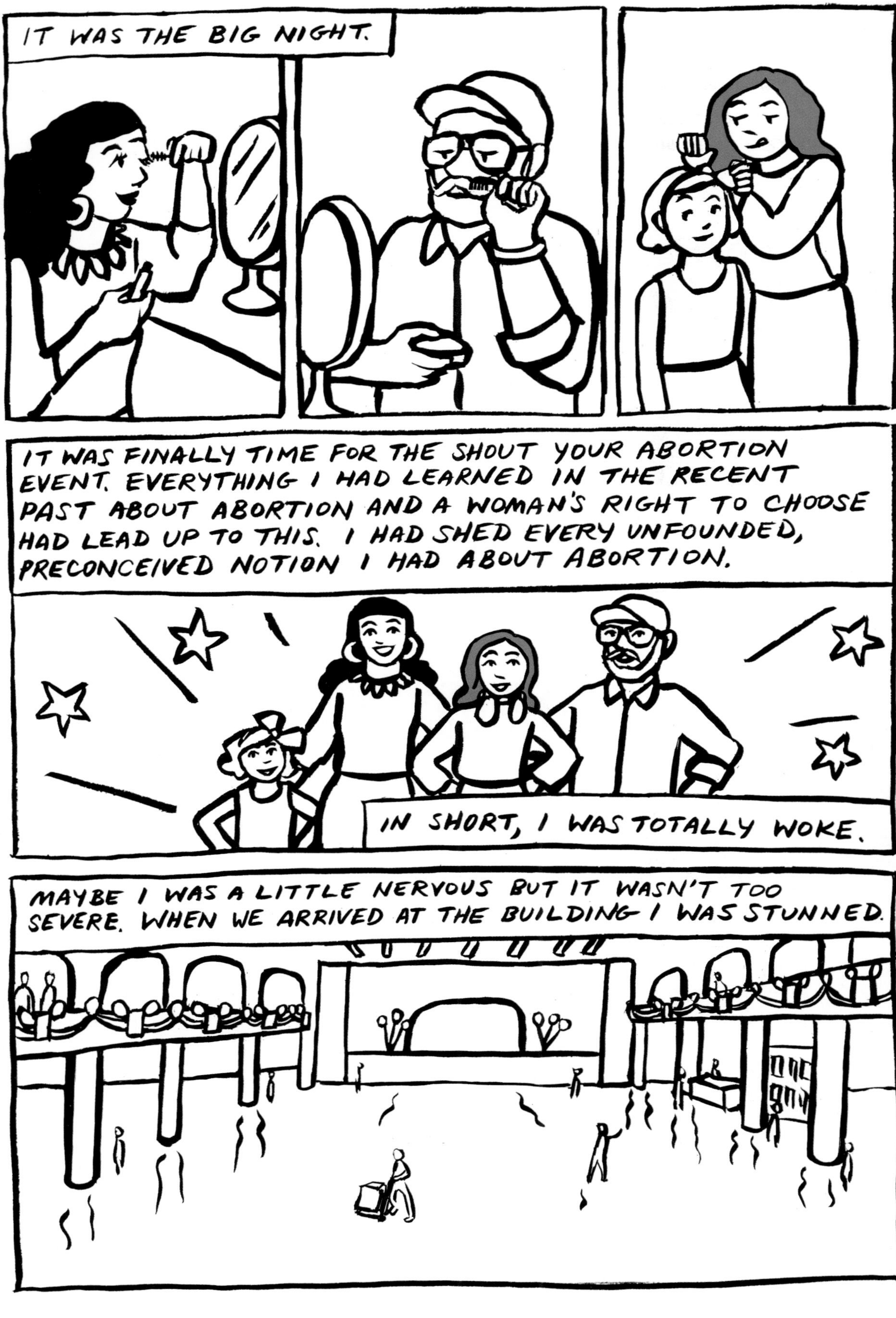
IT WAS THE BIG NIGHT.
IT WAS FINALLY TIME FOR THE SHOUT YOUR ABORTION EVENT. EVERYTHING I HAD LEARNED IN THE RECENT PAST ABOUT ABORTION AND A WOMAN'S RIGHT TO CHOOSE HAD LEAD UP TO THIS. I HAD SHED EVERY UNFOUNDED, PRECONCEIVED NOTION I HAD ABOUT ABORTION.
IN SHORT, I WAS TOTALLY WOKE.
MAYBE I WAS A LITTLE NERVOUS BUT IT WASN'T TOO SEVERE. WHEN WE ARRIVED AT THE BUILDING I WAS STUNNED.

NOT JUST BY THE ATMOSPHERE BUT BY EVERYTHING THIS EVENT REPRESENTED. ALL THESE PEOPLE HAD COME TOGETHER IN FAVOR OF A GOOD CAUSE. IT WAS INSPIRING!
Did you hear that the world is ending? Right here right where we stand
TACO CAT
at least no one's pretending like that would even be bad
Ohh, made it through the winter Whoa, summer too warm I wouldn't live anywhere else but don't say you weren't warned
Ooooh, beautiful Seattle Ahh, fall into the sea Earthquake, tsunami There's still no place I'd rather be
Earthquake, tsunami there's still no place I'd rather be
Can you see the neighborhood is ending? Reptiles take it in stride It's still worth defending Outside yelling at the tide
Uh oh, top left-hand corner Evacuation route Hard science, hard changes, no substitute!

CHAPTER 10:

FIND YOUR PATH

THE NIGHT WAS GOING SWIMMINGLY, UNTIL I NOTICED A BUNCH OF BALLOONS THAT HAD ALL FLOATED UP TO THE CEILING TOGETHER. I DON'T KNOW WHY BUT IT MADE ME UPSET. ALL OF THEM STUCK TOGETHER LIKE THAT. I KNOW THAT BALLOONS DON'T REALLY HAVE FEELINGS, BUT IT BUMMED ME OUT. MAYBE BECAUSE THOSE BALLOONS LOOKED THE SAME WAY I HAD OFTEN FELT. TRAPPED. STIFLED. STUCK. THEY DIDN'T GET TO FLOAT OFF INTO THEIR OWN CORNERS; THEY HAD TO STAY TOGETHER. BUT WHY? WHY WAS THAT THE WAY IT HAD TO BE? WHY COULDN'T THEY FIND THEIR OWN PLACE THAT WAS RIGHT FOR THEM? WHEN I WAS 7, I GOT KICKED OUT OF MY ELEMENTARY SCHOOL, PATHFINDER, BECAUSE I COULDN'T READ AND I WAS ACTING OUT DUE TO FRUSTRATION. THE SCHOOL TOLD MY MOTHER THAT IF I WASN'T ABLE TO TURN MY BEHAVIOR AROUND IN 30 DAYS THEY'D KICK ME OUT. MY MOTHER WAS HAVING NONE OF THAT, SO SHE PULLED ME OUT AND HOMESCHOOLED ME FOR THE REST OF THE YEAR. I DIDN'T FIND OUT HER MOTIVATIONS FOR PULLING ME OUT OF SCHOOL UNTIL YEARS LATER, BUT I KNEW THAT I DIDN'T BELONG THERE. I NEEDED TO FIND SOMEWHERE I DID BELONG. SO THEN I WENT TO LOUISA BOREN STEM K-8, WHICH SUITED ME BETTER, BUT I WAS STILL NEVER REALLY ACCEPTED. IT WASN'T UNTIL I GOT TO HIGH SCHOOL THAT I FINALLY STARTED TO FEEL LIKE I WAS WHERE I BELONGED. NO MATTER WHAT SITUATION, YOU HAVE TO DO WHAT'S RIGHT FOR YOU. AND THAT COULD MEAN GETTING AN ABORTION, KEEPING A BABY, GIVING UP A CHILD FOR ADOPTION, ADOPTING A CHILD, USING A SURROGATE, FREEZING YOUR EGGS, GETTING A HYSTERECTOMY, CHOOSING TO HAVE CHILDREN, CHOOSING NOT TO HAVE CHILDREN, SWITCHING SCHOOLS, CHANGING CAREERS, OR LIVING YOUR LIFE THE WAY YOU ALWAYS HAVE. EVERY PATH YOU TAKE LEADS YOU SOMEWHERE DIFFERENT AND EVERY CHOICE YOU MAKE HAS AN IMPACT. THAT'S WHY IT'S IMPORTANT TO FIND YOUR OWN PATH.

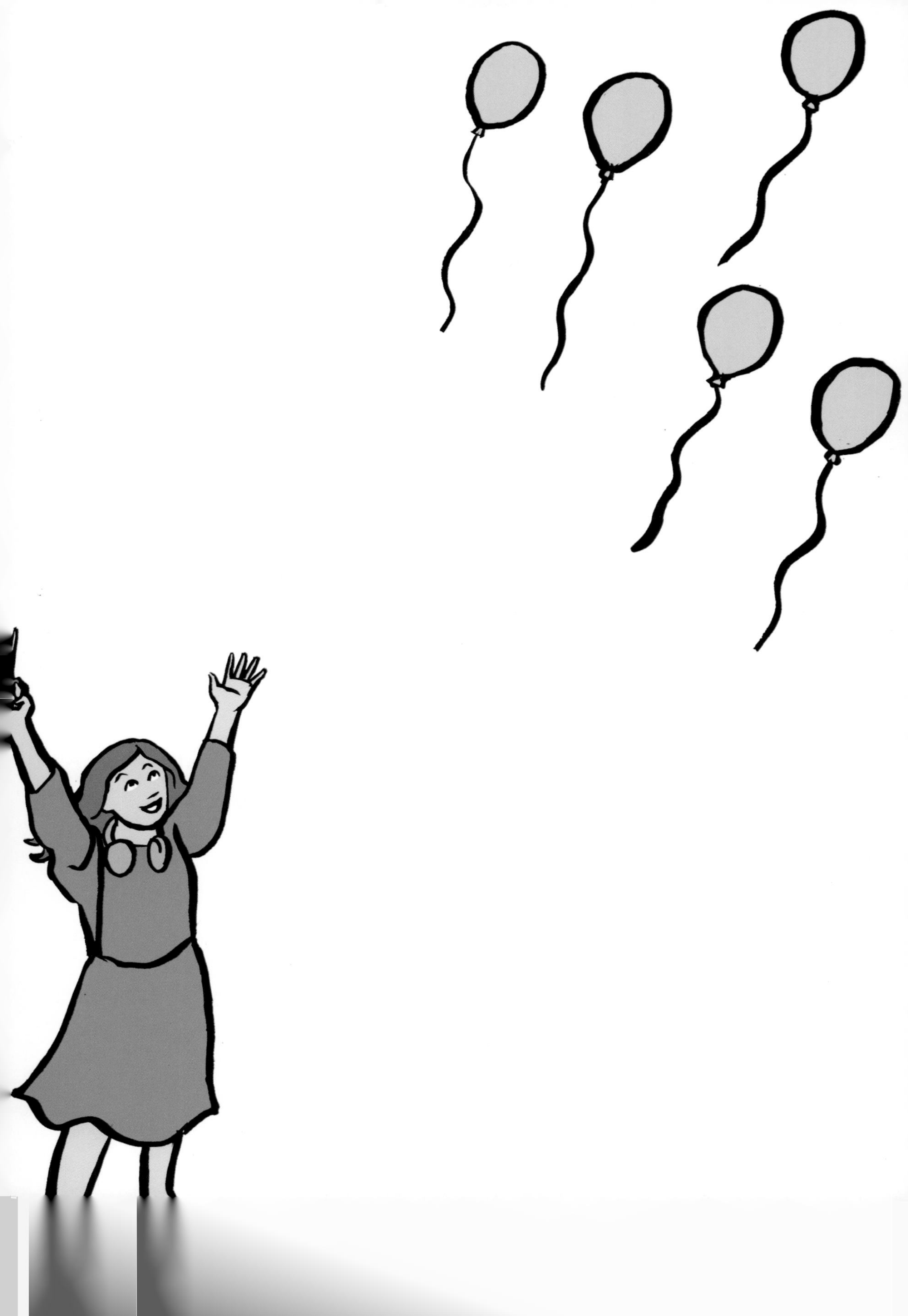

Postscript

Amelia Bonow

I usually say that Shout Your Abortion started as a viral hashtag, but that's not totally accurate; the status update I wrote about my abortion in 2015 was the public culmination of lots of conversations I'd been having with friends in private. We'd been talking about our abortions and how weird it was that we'd never talked about them before. And then, all of a sudden, we just *did*, and the world changed forever because that's how that works. Every tectonic cultural shift begins with a few people realizing that "the way things are" is a fake concept made up by people who want us to behave a certain way, and that we can actually do things differently, starting right this moment. Pretty soon, it's not just you (it never was). And poof! before you know it "the way things are" becomes "the way things used to be."

SYA is a movement that comprises countless people all over the world who have decided to talk about their abortions however they want, as opposed to how they're supposed to, which is that they're not. SYA is a million different instances of self-expression, of people deciding to move differently from here on out. At this point, enough of us have started moving differently that in some places, in some circles, this new way of moving just looks normal.

This book is a documentation of what it looked like when Beezus B. Murphy decided to trace her own assumptions to their origins and ask herself whether or not those assumptions were worthy of becoming beliefs. Beezus didn't grow up in a world free of abortion stigma, but, unlike many of us, she became aware of an alternative before all that other shit had the chance to put down roots.

Ideology is often invisible; it doesn't really feel like something we're opting into unless we can see other people opting out, and only then can it feel like a choice. I'm so proud that SYA helped illustrate that choice for Beezus, and it's an honor to help share her story of opting out—not just of abortion stigma but of compulsory heterosexuality, of being quiet, and of all sorts of prescribed modes of thinking and showing up in the world. It's easy for adults to see somebody like Beezus and be, like, "Wow! Some people are just born remarkable!" In part, yes, totally. But also, I think it's more convenient for us to believe that some people are born remarkable than it is to believe that people are capable of remarkable transformation.

This book is a great reminder that becoming who we are is a series of choices. There is nobody in this galaxy like Beezus B. Murphy, and obviously she was born remarkable, but Beezus B. Murphy is actively in the process of choosing to be exactly who she is, and I imagine that process will go on forever. Beezus decided to document some of that process in this book, in part because she knows that liberation is contagious, and she believes that we'd all be better off if we were free.

I met Beezus at the Stomp the Patriarchy Ball. I'd noticed the Murphy-Peetz family because of their advanced fashion, and also because Beezus and Minnow were 12 and 6 years old at the time. As I watched the two of them make the scene, my head was spinning at the implications of kids that age attending a big, wild, beautiful *abortion party*. I remember watching Beezus ricochet around the dancefloor in headphones and no shoes and realizing that it was now literally impossible for this person to grow up believing the lies about abortion that so many of us absorb: that abortions are mistakes, that if you feel fine about your abortion you're a total freak, that you are alone.

I watched this young powerful stranger zing around the entire night, and I knew that I was watching somebody's field of vision expand in a permanent way, and that made me super happy and proud, and I just thought, "I hope I get to see how that turns out!"

This book was illustrated by Tatiana Gill. Tatiana makes comics and illustrations that explore mental illness, addiction and recovery, body

Shout Your ABORTION!
THIS IS NOT A DEBATE.
KELLY O

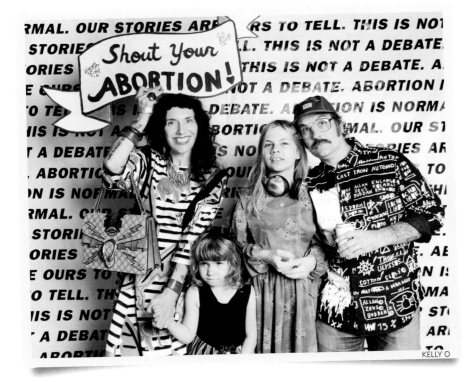

positivity, systems of oppression, depression, grief, and suicide. Her work is joyful and challenging and often both; her topical lane is wide, but her work often explores the parts of life that we aren't supposed to talk about.

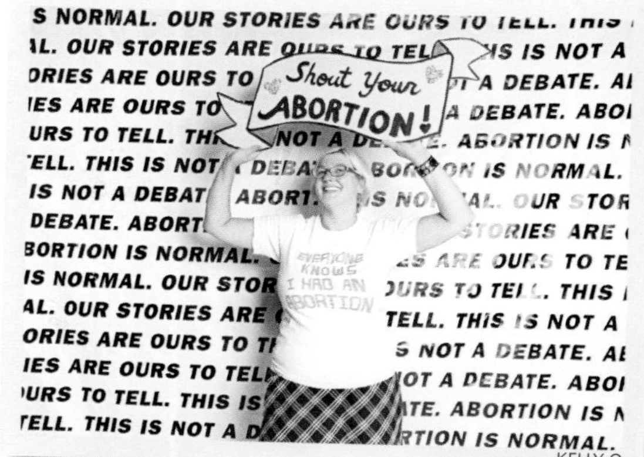
Shout Your ABORTION!
EVERYONE KNOWS I HAD AN ABORTION
KELLY O

A long time ago, Tatiana had an abortion. It was a complicated, not great situation; years after the fact, her abortion was something she'd never really processed with herself or other people, and which continued to hurt her immensely. Then one day #ShoutYourAbortion started trending, and Tatiana learned that tons of people have abortions and feeling bad isn't mandatory. In the years since, Tatiana has attended SYA rallies and events and marched around in a shirt that says, "EVERYONE KNOWS I HAD AN ABORTION," which caused strangers to hug her. She made a tough, gorgeous comic about her abortion, which appears in her excellent book *Wombgenda*. Finding her way into SYA changed Tatiana's whole life, and I can't even imagine how many peoples' lives Tatiana's work has changed since then—especially because *those* people will then start moving differently, and on and on and on, and before you know it that number is infinity. I highly recommend finding Tatiana on Instagram @TatsGill, and you can support her via Patreon.

The Stomp the Patriarchy Ball was SYA's first birthday celebration, and it was the best party I've ever been to. The bill was stacked with hometown heroes at the top of their game, the venue was decorated like an abortion fever dream occurring inside one of those cakes with the white frosting and the rainbow balls, and the whole evening was completely electric, because we all knew that we were experiencing something together that had never happened before.

The next morning, I went back to the venue by myself to clean up. I walked into the main room and stood there thinking about what had happened the night before. I just knew we'd fucking crushed it, and I cried. All the pink balloons had floated to the ceiling except for one, which was sitting in the center of the dance floor, just doing its thing.

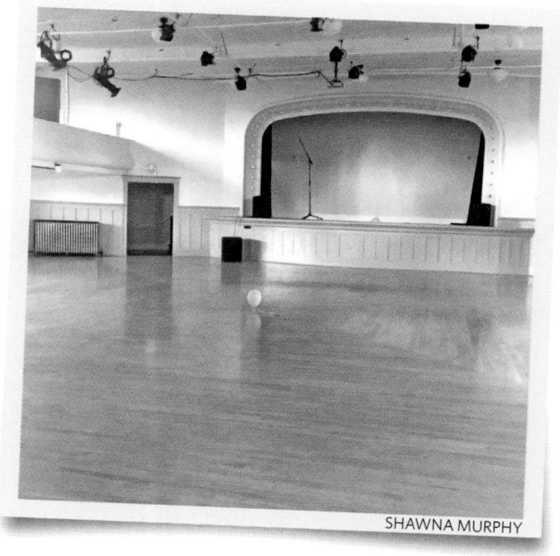
SHAWNA MURPHY

About the Contributors

SHAWNA MURPHY

Beezus B. Murphy, born 2004, is a Seattle-based dyslexic, asexual, lesbian, feminist, writer, and activist. She lives in Seattle with her mother Shawna Murphy, father Christian Peetz, younger sister Minnow Murphy, three pugs, two Siamese cats, and one Chihuahua. Her hobbies include the creation and consumption of media, roller skating, and trying to keep up in school. Beezus struggled in school and didn't learn how to read until she was eight because of her learning disability, but her kindergarten teacher Jennifer Nieman always said that when she did the world would lose her to books. It did, in some ways, but Beezus was far more consumed in many worlds of her own creation. Thanks to the influence of a Christian-propaganda show disguising itself as a teen drama, put haphazardly on Netflix where anyone could find it, Beezus accidentally became antiabortion for a few months. However, thanks to her proabortion feminist mom Shawna, she quickly recovered and sought to write a book about her journey.

Tatiana Gill is a Seattle cartoonist drawing about social and reproductive justice, mental health and addiction, and body positivity.

Tatiana has been creating comic books for twenty-five years. Her recent books include *Wombgenda*, *Blackoutings*, the *Fat Positive Coloring Book*, and *Recovery*. She contributes to publications across the world and has illustrated several books. Her work appears in galleries and exhibits around Seattle. Tatiana creates comics for a number of local organizations including Seattle/King County Health Department, Community Lunch, People's Harm Reduction Alliance, and Shout Your Abortion. Find her online at @tatsgill on instagram and Twitter and at tatianagill.com.

"From *Calvin and Hobbes* to *Wonder Woman*, comics have been an integral part of culture in the twentieth century. What's exciting is the way artists like Gill are using them as a tool to help policymakers understand the perspectives of those who are underrepresented in mainstream media."

—Lauren Himiak for *Rewire News Group*

Shout Your Abortion

Shout Your Abortion is a movement working to normalize abortion through art, media, and community events across the US and beyond. *My Mom Had an Abortion* is SYA's second book published with PM Press. SYA's eponymously titled first book—a collection of stories, art, and a tool kit for action—currently sits in the waiting and recovery rooms of hundreds of abortion clinics all over the country. Learn more about SYA and get involved at ShoutYourAbortion.com.

About PM Press

PM Press is an independent, radical publisher of books and media to educate, entertain, and inspire. Founded in 2007 by a small group of people with decades of publishing, media, and organizing experience, PM Press amplifies the voices of radical authors, artists, and activists. Our aim is to deliver bold political ideas and vital stories to all walks of life and arm the dreamers to demand the impossible. We have sold millions of copies of our books, most often one at a time, face to face. We're old enough to know what we're doing and young enough to know what's at stake. Join us to create a better world.

PM Press
PO Box 23912
Oakland, CA 94623
www.pmpress.org

PM Press in Europe
europe@pmpress.org
www.pmpress.org.uk

Friends of PM Press

These are indisputably momentous times—the financial system is melting down globally and the Empire is stumbling. Now more than ever there is a vital need for radical ideas.

In the years since its founding—and on a mere shoestring—PM Press has risen to the formidable challenge of publishing and distributing knowledge and entertainment for the struggles ahead. With over 450 releases to date, we have published an impressive and stimulating array of literature, art, music, politics, and culture. Using every available medium, we've succeeded in connecting those hungry for ideas and information to those putting them into practice.

Friends of PM allows you to directly help impact, amplify, and revitalize the discourse and actions of radical writers, filmmakers, and artists. It provides us with a stable foundation from which we can build upon our early successes and provides a much-needed subsidy for the materials that can't necessarily pay their own way. You can help make that happen—and receive every new title automatically delivered to your door once a month—by joining as a Friend of PM Press. And, we'll throw in a free T-shirt when you sign up.

Here are your options:

- **$30 a month** Get all books and pamphlets plus 50% discount on all webstore purchases

- **$40 a month** Get all PM Press releases (including CDs and DVDs) plus 50% discount on all webstore purchases

- **$100 a month** Superstar—Everything plus PM merchandise, free downloads, and 50% discount on all webstore purchases

For those who can't afford $30 or more a month, we have **Sustainer Rates** at $15, $10, and $5. Sustainers get a free PM Press T-shirt and a 50% discount on all purchases from our website.

Your Visa or Mastercard will be billed once a month, until you tell us to stop. Or until our efforts succeed in bringing the revolution around. Or the financial meltdown of Capital makes plastic redundant. Whichever comes first.

Shout Your Abortion

Edited by Amelia Bonow and Emily Nokes with a Foreword by Lindy West

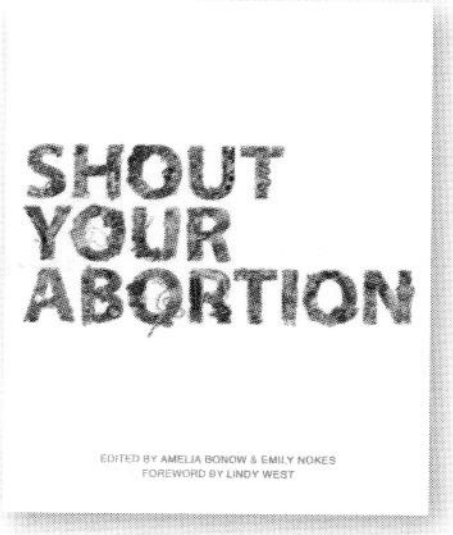
SHOUT YOUR ABORTION

ISBN: 978-1-62963-573-6
$24.95 256 pages

Following the U.S. Congress's attempts to defund Planned Parenthood, the hashtag #ShoutYourAbortion became a viral conduit for abortion storytelling, receiving extensive media coverage and positioning real human experiences at the center of America's abortion debate for the very first time. The online momentum sparked a grassroots movement that has subsequently inspired countless individuals to share their abortion stories in art, media, and community events all over the country, and to begin building platforms for others to do the same.

Shout Your Abortion is a collection of photos, essays, and creative work inspired by the movement of the same name, a template for building new communities of healing, and a call to action. Since SYA's inception, people all over the country have shared stories and begun organizing in a range of ways: making art, hosting comedy shows, creating abortion-positive clothing, altering billboards, starting conversations that had never happened before. This book documents some of these projects and illuminates the individuals who have breathed life into this movement, illustrating the profound liberatory and political power of defying shame and claiming sole authorship of our experiences. With *Roe vs. Wade* on the brink of reversal, the act of shouting one's abortion has become explicitly radical, and *Shout Your Abortion* is needed more urgently than ever before.

A More Graceful Shaboom

Jacinta Bunnell
Illustrated by Crystal Vielula

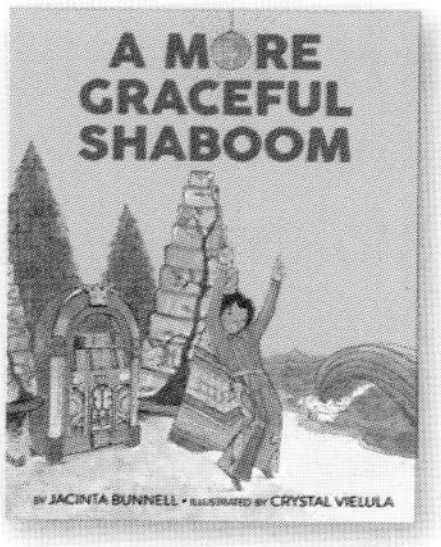
A MORE GRACEFUL SHABOOM

ISBN: 978-1-62963-824-9
$16.95 48 pages

A gender nonbinary protagonist named Harmon Jitney finds their joy and purpose in a magical satchel which leads to an extraordinary, previously undiscovered universe. This book features LGBTQAI+ characters seamlessly woven into a delightful, imagination-sparking story, without overtly being a lesson book about gender and sexual orientation. Follow Harmon as they unlock the key to their own inner happiness and sense of community.

"It's often been said that you can't be it, unless you see it, but the queer youth of today are often busy being whatever it is by the time they finally see it represented out there in the world. The classification they choose or the person with whom they identify presents itself as an affirmation rather than an inspiration. A More Graceful Shaboom *is a major affirmation to anyone who identifies as non-binary—and an inspiration to us all."*
—James Lecesne, co-founder of the Trevor Project

"A More Graceful Shaboom *is what would happen if Remy Charlip and Freddy Mercury had a baby. It's what would happen if you could live in Narnia and Woodstock at the same time. It's what would happen if the idea of inclusiveness was taken to the outer edges of the universe. There's room enough for everyone, plus there's a disco ball. That's enough for me."*
—Brian Selznick, author and illustrator of *The Invention of Hugo Cabret*

(H)afrocentric Comics: Volumes 1–4

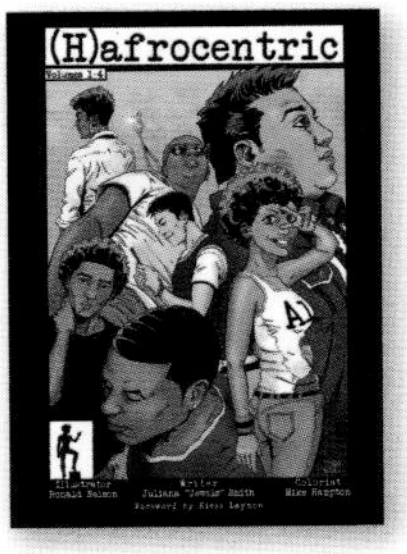
(H)afrocentric

Juliana "Jewels" Smith, illustrated by Ronald Nelson, with colors/lettering by Mike Hampton, and a foreword by Kiese Laymon

ISBN: 978-1-62963-448-7
$20.00 136 pages

Glyph Award winner Juliana "Jewels" Smith and illustrator Ronald Nelson have created an unflinching visual and literary tour-de-force on the most pressing issues of the day— including gentrification, police violence, and the housing crisis—with humor and biting satire. *(H) afrocentric* tackles racism, patriarchy, and popular culture head-on. Unapologetic and unabashed, *(H)afrocentric* introduces us to strong yet vulnerable students of color, as well as an aesthetic that connects current Black pop culture to an organic reappropriation of hip hop fashion circa the early 90s.

We start the journey when gentrification strikes the neighborhood surrounding Ronald Reagan University. Naima Pepper recruits a group of disgruntled undergrads of color to combat the onslaught by creating and launching the first and only anti-gentrification social networking site, mydiaspora.com. The motley crew is poised to fight back against expensive avocado toast, muted Prius cars, exorbitant rent, and cultural appropriation. Whether Naima and the gang are transforming social media, leading protests, fighting rent hikes, or working as "Racial Translators," the students at Ronald Reagan University take movements to a new level by combining their tech-savvy, Black Millennial sensibilities with their individual backgrounds, goals, and aspirations.

"Smith's comics ooze with originality."
—AFROPUNK

Crossroads: I Live Where I Like: A Graphic History

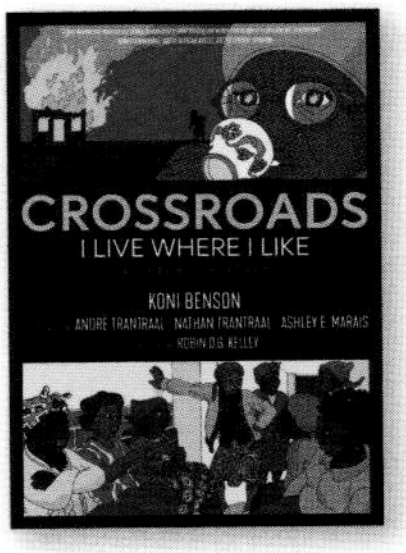
CROSSROADS
I LIVE WHERE I LIKE
KONI BENSON

Koni Benson. Illustrated byAndré Trantraal, Nathan Trantraal, and Ashley E. Marais, and with a Foreword by Robin D.G. Kelley

ISBN: 978-1-62963-835-5
$20.00 168 pages

Drawn by South African political cartoonists the Trantraal brothers and Ashley Marais, *Crossroads: I Live Where I Like* is a graphic nonfiction history of women-led movements at the forefront of the struggle for land, housing, water, education, and safety in Cape Town over half a century. Drawing on over sixty life narratives, it tells the story of women who built and defended Crossroads, the only informal settlement that successfully resisted the apartheid bulldozers in Cape Town. The story follows women's organized resistance from the peak of apartheid in the 1970s to ongoing struggles for decent shelter today. Importantly, this account was workshopped with contemporary housing activists and women's collectives who chose the most urgent and ongoing themes they felt spoke to and clarified challenges against segregation, racism, violence, and patriarchy standing between the legacy of the colonial and apartheid past and a future of freedom still being fought for.

Presenting dramatic visual representations of many personalities and moments in the daily life of this township, the book presents a thoughtful and thorough chronology, using archival newspapers, posters, photography, pamphlets, and newsletters to further illustrate the significance of the struggles at Crossroads for the rest of the city and beyond. This collaboration has produced a beautiful, captivating, accessible, forgotten, and in many ways uncomfortable history of Cape Town that has yet to be acknowledged.